PRAISE FOR MATT GEIGER:

"Geiger whittles down the pomp and pretension of life's circumstances and trains his philosopher's vision on the most basic of human questions. With an often self-deprecating humor and more accuracy than any scientific instrument, he launches his stories into the dark and tender places of our being."
—Kimberly Blaeser, author of Apprenticed to Justice

"[R]aises humor to a new level."
—Michael Tidemann, Writers and Writing

"Radiates humor and insight."
—The Capital Times

"I devoured Humorist/Philosopher Matt Geiger's new book like a fresh batch of hot, buttered popcorn."   —The St. Augustine Record

"The best way to read this book is to just let go and follow Geiger wherever his fancy takes him."   —The Pioneer Press

"By turns poignant and hilarious, his witty, empathetic observations of fatherhood, family, and community evoke laughter and touch the heart in equal measure."
—Jennifer Chiaverini, New York Times bestselling author

"[A]n author with an impressive flair for originality and deftly crafted storytelling."
—Midwest Book Review

"Geiger delves into the heart of common experience with wit, humility, and vivid detail. Highly recommended."
—Kathleen Ernst, bestselling author

"The world needs to know about Matt Geiger."
—Doug Moe, Madison Magazine

"Matt Geiger's work is brilliant, varied and heartbreaking as the best works of Dostoyevsky, Hemingway, and Grizzard. Okay, mostly Grizzard. Except without the ex-wives. But it's funny stuff, really, and it's filled with genuine heart."
—Alex Bledsoe, author of The Hum and the Shiver

"Geiger's writing is a thrilling discovery. You feel as though you're standing in a queue somewhere and all of a sudden you chat up the stranger next to you, who you realize inside of three sentences is just a fascinating, ridiculously fun individual. His work is simply brimming with wit and insight. A truly modern American storyteller!"
—Kirsten Lobe, author of Paris Hangover

"This extraordinary collection is captivating, fun and memorable, and it deserves a large audience."   —Nick Chiarkas, author of Weepers

ASTONISHING TALES!*

STORIES & ESSAYS

YOUR ASTONISHMENT MAY VARY

Other books by Matt Geiger:

The Geiger Counter: Raised by Wolves and Other Stories

ASTONISHING TALES!*

STORIES & ESSAYS

*YOUR ASTONISHMENT MAY VARY

MATT GEIGER

HENSCHELHAUS PUBLISHING, INC.
MILWAUKEE, WISCONSIN

Copyright © 2019 by Matt Geiger
All rights reserved.

Some names and locations have been changed.

Published by
HenschelHAUS Publishing, Inc.
www.henschelHAUSbooks.com

ISBN (hardcover): 978159598-666-5
ISBN (paperback): 978159598-667-2
ISBN (audio): 978159598-669-6
E-ISBN: 978159598-668-0

LCCN: 2018954834

PCIP: PENDING

Cover photo of Bonnie Logan (1961) used by permission from
Adam Reader, Knight Publishing Corp. Los Angeles, CA

"The metaphysicians ... do not seek for the truth or even for verisimilitude, but rather for the astounding."

Jorge Luis Borges

For Greta

CONTENTS

CREDITS

The following stories originally appeared in the cited publications:

- "Everyday Easter Eggs" originally appeared in *The Sunlight Press* (as "Anytime We Want") (thesunlightpress.com)

- "The Cave" originally appeared in *Northerly* (livenortherly.com)

- "Boring Death," "Existential Christmas," and "Astonishing" originally appeared on Wisconsin Public Radio (wisconsinlife.org)

- "Chickens of the Apocalypse" and "Little Dipper Boy" originally appeared in *Journal From the Heartland* (journalfromtheheartland.com)

- "The Night Chang Died," "Axe Man," "Floyd," "This Was Written by a Neanderthal," "Coffee," "Tantrums," "Dandelions," "Meh, Not So Funny," and "Matt Geiger is Dead" originally appeared in *News Publishing Co.* newspapers.

MATT GEIGER IS DEAD

"**L**oathing Matt Geiger is so damn easy." That's a real headline on a popular blog.

"Is Matt Geiger black?" It's a topic of heated, though not particularly nuanced debate.

These are the things I have to read when I Google myself.

I'm not the most famous Matt Geiger. I haven't been since at least 1992, when I was 12 years old and a guy who shared my name was drafted into the NBA. The following day, someone left a little envelope in my locker.

"Oooh, a love note from a girl!" I thought excitedly. Pulling the paper pouch down from the shelf, I saw a portion of a newspaper sports section fall out and corkscrew erratically to the ground.

"Oh, no, it's just some sports news," I thought, with a small slump of my shoulders as I picked it up and read it. It was about the NBA draft. Someone had circled "Matt Geiger," the name of a player selected by the Miami Heat. I thought it wouldn't significantly impact my life. I was wrong.

Many years later, when I was 37 and my first book came out, my publisher had me sign up to receive alerts whenever my name is mentioned in the press. I imagined the enthusiastic little "ding" my phone makes when I receive a message, followed by a series of articles by critics who said I was "the next Michael Perry" or "like the hilarious and talented lovechild of David Sedaris and Bill Bryson." I'm still waiting for those notifications, although Mr. Perry really did refer to my debut, and this was one of the proudest moments of my life, as "a book."

What I usually get is a peppering of stories about advanced basketball analytics, and nostalgic retrospectives about the 2001 NBA Finals, usually with a headline like, "Matt Geiger reflects on losing on the NBA's biggest stage."

Matt, who stands a full foot closer to the heavens than I do, was a solid pro with a long career. I've had my breath taken away several times when I inadvertently stumbled upon headlines about his life, and mistook him for me.

There was the time, shortly after the dawn of the new millennium, when I, an increasingly flabby and sedentary college student, was forced to sit out several games for steroid use.

Then I built a 28,000-square-foot mansion in the Tampa Bay area. It had six bedrooms and eight bathrooms because, while I only want half a dozen people resting in my house at any given moment, I need to make sure at least two more than that can urinate, all at the exact same time. While the bedrooms and bathrooms seemed excessive, even to me, the shark tank, which was also part of the house, was a rock solid idea. It wasn't practical in the manner of a walk-in food pantry or a place to hang coats by the doorway, but it was pretty much required that I keep dangerous and exotic animals in a domestic setting once my career as a professional athlete came to an end. I suspect such language might even be written into most athletes' contracts. Or perhaps, on your last day as a heavyweight boxer or NFL wide receiver, you simply receive a nice watch and a baby Amur tiger.

My advisors in college regularly warned me that writing and philosophy are not traditionally sources of lavish income. Imagine their surprise when they read in a magazine about my artificial lake stocked with 2,500 bass, or my personal herd of bison, Watusi cattle, donkeys, and a single miniature horse. (When I read about the horse, I couldn't help thinking, "At this point, why not just go crazy and get two?")

It's strange to look yourself up online and learn you have 40 televisions in your home, 18 of which are directly linked to video game consoles. It's weird to worry that maybe, on second thought, you don't have enough bathrooms for all the people who come over to play Xbox. It's bizarre to get genuinely mad at county officials when you read they won't let you install your own private helicopter pad in the backyard, due to some silly zoning regulations.

None of these emotions compares to the way I felt when I learned Matt Geiger owed $290,000 in back taxes, or the genuine chagrin with which I greeted the following headline (in the *Tampa Bay Times*) in 2011: "Matt Geiger's mansion finally sells—at a big discount."

Fuck, I thought, *even my fantasy version of myself is bad with money.*

Then something worse occurred to me.

"What will happen to my donkeys?"

Reading that the bigger, richer, more successful version of myself had fallen into a pit of economic despair was like being Clark Kent and learning Superman has really bad degenerative arthritis. This is what it's like to discover the knight you're pretending to be in a daydream has crippling seasonal allergies and can't go dragon hunting because there's simply too much mucus.

I really am incredibly absent-minded. I forget appointments, and my daily car key hunt has become something of a glum ritual in my house. I'm an agnostic, so I don't pray to God often, but when I do, I usually ask the Divine Creator and Prime Mover to help me find my socks or wallet. I'm even able to lose a remote control without ever rising from the couch, which is, perhaps, a special kind of talent.

I frequently forget major life events, and I always try to forget that I once moved from Florida to New Jersey, which is like clearing up your malaria with a nice case of bird flu. The point is, I'm accustomed to remembering things about myself, things I had previously forgotten, so I often wonder, just for a moment, if maybe I really did fall behind on my taxes, or get screwed by county officials who were merely jealous of my helicopter and its need for an adequate place to land.

A popular national magazine based out of New York once contacted me and asked that I track down a local Midwestern man named Johnny Depp. They were doing a piece about ordinary people who share names with celebrities. When I found the guy's address and went to his apartment building, I encountered a level of squalor that gave me pause. Perhaps highlighting the differences between these two men—their jobs, their lovers, their incomes, their bone structure, and whether or not their eyes twinkled—would be unintentionally cruel? We might as well put an elderly alley cat with mange right next to a robust lion, photograph them, then point out to readers all over the country that one cat is actually much better than the other.

Standing there, I realized what the magazine had really directed me to do: Ask the one whose life is demonstrably worse in every aspect what it's like to live in a cruel, ironic universe.

Through the apartment's hollow door, I heard someone haranguing Mr. Depp. So I walked away without ringing the bell. A couple years later, I read that Johnny Depp (the movie star) had run into serious financial and marital problems, and I considered returning, now that their lifestyles were likely more similar. Then I forgot all about it, just like I sometimes forget I didn't score 5,059 points during my NBA career.

Sometimes I wonder if maybe the Matt Geiger who played basketball ever Googles himself and finds something about me, instead. Maybe he was confused when he read that he penned a collection of essays. Or perhaps he nodded his enormous, shaven head and empathized when he read criticism of me.

I don't know. I tried to reach the other Matt Geiger. I got as far as his twin brother, Mark, with whom I spoke on the phone in 2017. He was friendly, and he told me he'd relay the message to his brother. I never heard back.

The Internet masses are obsessed with race, gender, and political affiliation. It was only a matter of time before I received an alert directing me to a blog thread in which people engaged in fierce debate about whether Matt Geiger is black or white. Some wrote that he is white, possibly because he is. Others argued with conviction that he is African American, defending their position with various statistics and metrics that indicated he was simply too good to be white. Larry Bird inevitably came up, as did Spike Lee, and that's about the time I realized they weren't talking about me, I was late for work, and I really needed to put my phone in my pocket and start looking for my keys.

"That's enough Internet for today," I muttered as I walked out the door.

The headline I really don't want to read hasn't been written yet: "Matt Geiger has died."

I know it would fill me with despair to get an enthusiastic little "ding" on my phone and be greeted with those words. Reading of my own demise would inevitably lead to a deep depression, but it's unlikely for ontological reasons. Reading about the death of someone else—in this case someone who appears to be genuinely nice and with whom I'm somehow linked—might also ruin my day.

The alternative is not much better. It's that one morning, a retired basketball player will read that some other guy has died. Someone with whom he shares a name and a deep affection for miniature horses.

Either way, Matt Geiger will be dead. Long live Matt Geiger.

EVERYDAY EASTER EGGS

She had the drill again.

"Is this too loud for yoga, Mom?!" Hadley, our two-year-old daughter, belted over its roar. Her fat, thick feet skidded to a stop when they left the slick faux hardwood and snagged in the matted, yellow shag carpeting. It's one of those little lines of demarcation that give our domestic world its contours. A place where synthetic brown planks are engulfed in the doorway by fiery nylon tufts. For a toddler, it's a lesson in surface friction. For adults, it serves as a reminder of the vast aesthetic excesses of the 1970s.

"IS THIS TOO LOUD FOR YOGA?!"

Unpredictable curls of hair bounced like springs in her face as she grasped the power tool. It was a toy, but was as loud as the real thing. It sounded like a garbage disposal struggling to choke down a rack of beef ribs.

My wife was in front of the television following the instructions given forcefully by the contortionist on the screen. "Warrior Pose." "Downward Facing Dog." "Inside Out Bonobo."

Taking her finger off the trigger just long enough to squeeze in another sentence of her own, Hadley suddenly adopted the rolling, countrified voice of a portly southern sheriff: "Awww, mah mom don't like it..."

Then she turned, fired up the power tool again, and sprinted away in the more happy, much faster cousin of a galumph. I could tell by the way the sound oscillated between loud and quiet that she was running from room to room.

It was the second time in a week that she, a little girl who has never been south of Illinois, suddenly began speaking in a syrupy southern drawl. The first time, she was seated naked in the bathtub. Our little gray cat, lost in pleasant speculation about where to throw up next, wandered into the bathroom. He suddenly saw the child and the water, was filled with visible horror, and bolted.

"Awwww!" Hadley lamented. "Mah cat don't take a bayath." She sounded like the kind of person who gives sentimental Christian names to shotguns and pickup trucks—names like "Darlene" and "Lou Anne."

Perhaps our house had once been owned by an old southern general whose ghost was now floating around haunting the place, occasionally possessing my toddler. Demonic possession, I realized, would also explain several of her other, more erratic behaviors. Or maybe it was a genetic thing, like having a cleft palate or webbed toes.

I imagined a doctor returning to the examination room and sitting down with a somber look on her face. "We got the test results back," she would say with grim sincerity. "They're positive. I'm sorry, but your daughter is southern."

Every sentence my daughter utters is an adventure.

When she sees a flock of ducks, she'll point at them and smile. "What are the ducks doing?"

"They are swimming in the pond, honey."

Then she'll point to a cluster of men near the shore. "And what are the mans doing?"

"The men are fishing."

"Okay. And what are the fesh doing?"

"The fish," I say with a sigh, "are swimming. Or maybe fishes. I don't really know. Let's get away from the water."

The lesson is always the same—that English is confusing and inconsistent, just like everything else in life. Get used to it and enjoy it, I tell her. No one really knows nearly as much as they pretend to know.

She's never disappointed with an answer. And she appears perfectly content in the understanding that ignorance and wildly speculative guesses are just natural, healthy steps on the journey toward a better comprehension of the world—like the fact that you might have to turn left a few times on your cross-country trip, even though your final destination is on the right.

In the spring, we made Easter eggs with her, primarily as a way to kill an hour before the sun set—a time of day when I can turn on the television without feeling like a bad parent. It was Easter, after all, and that is traditionally when you boil and decorate bird embryos to celebrate the resurrection of an ancient, murdered god, and the impending visitation of a massive, generous rodent. Hadley loved it, squealing and laughing as she mixed the dyes together to create a shade of brown she is particularly fond of.

A few days later, as I pitched some kitchen scraps into the backyard for our chickens, she turned off her drill and looked up at me. Her hair was straight that day, according to its whims, but her eyes were as big, dark, and sincere as ever: "Dad, I want to make Easter eggs."

"We can't!" I said with the well-worn confidence of an imbecile. "We can only decorate eggs on…" It was at this point I realized I had no idea on what day Easter actually falls. "Well, it moves around, I think." After a brief consultation with my phone, I discovered Easter always takes place on the first Sunday following the Paschal Full Moon.

"What's Paschal Full Moon, Daddy?" she asked.

Rather than descending further down this particular rabbit hole, I decided to adapt my worldview.

"You know what? We CAN make Easter eggs. Also, sweetheart, I honestly have no idea what the Paschal Full Moon is."

"We," I said as my heart began thumping fervently in my chest, as if I were a general marching up and down before a line of warriors on some vast field of battle, "can decorate eggs anytime we want to!"

I dropped the Tupperware bowl I was holding. She discarded her drill. Then, we went inside and decorated all our eggs. It was one of the best mornings of my life—one of those rare days when you aren't just secretly biding your time until it's socially acceptable to drink beer, play video games, or go to sleep and try all over again the next morning. One of those events during which, if someone asked you what you'd rather be doing, you'd reply honestly: "Nothing in the world."

It's what parenting is all about—the chance to teach someone how to use verbs and toilets, while they teach you that most of the rules governing our lives are arbitrary and pointless. Many are simply relics from days when people had very different problems and priorities. Which side of the plate a knife goes on, when you can wear hats, and how tall your grass can be—these are ridiculous guidelines with no practical implications. People take them seriously simply because they are told to, and as they grew up, they stopped asking questions.

I often discover such rules were created to combat problems long ago swept away by the modern world. This one is so you won't catch polio, and that one is so you won't stub your toe on all the Tasmanian tigers lying around. Like the Great Wall of China, which has outlived the marauding Mongol hordes it was built to keep out, the solutions outlasted their corresponding problems.

So I'm rapidly letting go of all the inane, arbitrary rules that govern most adults' lives. Maybe it's because my daughter has shown me that being distant and glum, and taking work and politics too seriously, are guidelines you don't really need to follow. Or maybe it's just the sound of a little, orange, plastic power drill gradually driving me toward some kind of blissful insanity. All I know is that every sentence is an adventure, and every day comes with a chance of Easter eggs.

ASTONISHING

The billboard had promised gasoline, sandwiches, and the opportunity to see a two-headed calf named "Heady."

Standing in the rural gas station, I gazed up and scanned for signs it was a hoax. Maybe the deformity was evidence of a taxidermist's deft touch rather than the handiwork of a hilarious, but also cruel and uncaring god.

Unlike driving a car or working at the office, this deserved my full attention. I regularly scold myself for being disengaged from the majestic world around me. For slipping away mentally, and not taking note of the beauty when a raindrop shatters against the peeling planks of an old porch. For not being stunned by the mythic, atavistic form of a vast cloud of steam rising from the sagging jowls of a big dog on a sunny, midwinter afternoon.

It's strange, because when I was a child, I was sure I was Sherlock Holmes. I would lie on the top bunk, a few inches from the ceiling, reading about the dramatic, theatrically morbid high of living in Victorian London. The tales would whisk me away to a dark, claustrophobic world full of mutton chops, opium dens, and all the tweed, steaming horse manure, and untreated venereal disease you could ever want. I always experienced them as Holmes.

I, too, was aloof, eccentric, and misunderstood. I, too, was always the smartest person in the room. I always knew what was going on—I always saw the things around me, from killers lurking in the shadows to the dietary and social habits of those who merely played bit parts in the grand story swirling around me.

Then it happened. I was sitting in a room full of peach-colored desks and chairs, surrounded by the strange smells and sounds of other children my age. We played a game of deduction, and a boy named Calvin solved nearly every problem before I could even raise my hand.

"Way to go, Calvin!" the teacher shouted when it was over. "I guess we have our very own Sherlock Holmes here!"

That's when it struck me.

I wasn't Holmes.

I was Watson.

A sidekick. Someone who saw little, and understood less. Watson was always so astonished—a sure sign of stupidity, I thought. He admitted it out loud all the time: "Astonishing!"

I kept reading about Holmes, and after many years, I came to see things differently. Watson wasn't blind. He didn't see the things Holmes saw, of course. But he saw Holmes in his place at the center of a mysterious world. He saw it all with the meta-vision of any good author. After all, they were Watson's stories.

Maybe, I thought with a little grin, I am just like Watson, who wasn't dumb after all. Maybe I can look around and see two-headed calves, love, and beauty where other people do not. Perhaps, like him, I can be constantly amazed.

I did crack the case of the two-headed calf, at least. It belongs to a nice Midwestern couple who own the gas station. It was born alive on a nearby farm, but its back broke during the delivery. It experienced the world for a moment, then died, the glint vanishing from its four black eyes. Then they stuffed and mounted her heads.

As we chatted, Heady's current owner looked up at her and smiled. "We put antlers on her at Christmas," she said. They festoon the whole place with garlands and holiday cheer, and they never forget to make sure Heady is part of the celebration.

Something about the absurdity of it was beautiful. I smiled back, looked up at the calf again, and said the only word that came to mind: "Astonishing."

HORSE BABY

My daughter loves to empty all the shampoos, conditioners, and soaps when she takes a shower. It's not the monetary loss that bothers me. The problem—and you already know this if you have ever stepped naked into an oblong porcelain bowl in which every square inch has been coated in slick hair conditioner—is that it's probably how I'm going to die.

My ancestors were Vikings and proud Celtic warriors. While I'm not precisely sure how one earns entrance through the gates of Valhalla, I suspect "slipped on lavender-scented goo" does not qualify as dying with honor.

It's always the same: You set one foot in, then lift the other into the air at the exact moment you realize your first foot has refused to stay put, like a wanderlust-filled air hockey puck near a gusty window, perpetually floating in erratic directions. You quickly plant your second foot with additional force in the tub. Rather than stabilizing you, this simply amplifies the initial problem. As you go down, you grab a shower curtain, which is also coated in conditioner, and a big, plump fistful of air that, although it is not coated in anything slippery, is an apathetic god who refuses to come to your aid in this time of terrible need.

Lying there, covered in slime like some sci-fi space traveler emerging from a time-travel pod, you remember that getting up is actually the most difficult part of this ritual.

So you lie there, blinded by a stream of water from above, and you marvel at the chaos in your life. Is this normal? Do I have what it takes to make it through another day? Do I have what it takes to stand? To walk? To run?

Eventually you rise, and you stand there like a newborn foal, wet and on quivering legs, feeling the gravity of an entire planet on your back as you wait for the last of the conditioner to swirl down the drain. This is how you start your day. This is how you orient yourself to the world. This is your default setting. Naked and afraid, surrounded by empty plastic bottles as the last of the water slides down what has to be the most vigorously lubricated drain on the planet.

To make matters worse, you know you will reek of lavender or coconut oil for days.

You are the adult in this house. And this is where you are, stripped of your dignity and everything else as you wonder if you have what it takes to cultivate and maintain a good and meaningful life. A life in which everyone is relatively well fed, relatively clean, and relatively alive. It all falls on you, you worry, and you can't even maintain order in a bathtub, let alone your entire home, or the big, menacing, broiling world outside it.

The emotions flow through you. First confusion. Then anger. Then frustration. Then wild, exuberant laughter as you remember that this is not a rehearsal for something else; this is actually it! This is the immense, pressing reality of your life.

As we find ourselves out in the world, under those skies and face to face with anger, self-righteous pedantry and juvenile bigotry, we are more like that newborn foal than we first realized. The one you see drop to the earth, disoriented and covered in the viscous liquid of early life. The one you see rising on unsteady, spindly legs, despite the overwhelming weight of gravity upon its back. I grew up on a farm, so I know what happens next.

Because it wasn't the birth that I would rush to see when a baby horse was born. It wasn't the slimy plunge to the dirt below. It was what happened next that captivated me. The thing we rushed to see, and we had to rush because it happened so quickly, was what happened next.

The creature would stand uncertainly, and a moment later, its legs would stop shaking. It would take a couple steps out into a daunting world. Gravity would relent. The slime dried. And off it would gallop, running, jumping, and frolicking in the sun.

THE CAVE

Twenty-six thousand years ago, an eight-year-old boy and a brawny wolf-dog walked together along the wet clay floor of a dank, labyrinthine cave.

Their tracks, which hardened and froze in time, appear out of oblivion, continue for 45 meters, then vanish back into the eternally fertile haze of our imaginations. You can see where the boy, who was walking and not running, slipped in the clay, righted himself, and continued on before they disappeared. He carried a torch, which he stopped to rub against the rock wall, an ancient technique that prodded the flame to burn brighter against the darkness.

A child and his long-toothed friend, venturing together into the shadows in search of adventure, or food, or meaning.

That is all we know.

In the spaces between those facts, our minds flourish. In those spaces lives the very nature of our humanity.

I spent the last week thinking about this pair of explorers, wondering what those moments were like. Despite the passage of so many thousands of years, they were real. I wonder what they smelled like, what they thought, what they saw, and what they felt as they made their way through Pleistocene lives. Their world was inhabited by a menagerie of exotic, hungry beasts; giant European bears, hyenas, and lions.

On the walls of that same cave prior generations, nearly as ancient to the boy and the wolf-dog as the boy and the wolf-dog are to us, painted the animals they killed and ate, and the animals that killed and ate them. In the recesses of the cave, the skulls of bears wait patiently in the eternal silence of God or the lack thereof. Possibly placed there to signify their divinity. Maybe just resting where they were tossed or fell.

* * * * *

Parents in the year 2018 like to bicker about how best to raise children. Since about 99 percent of Internet chatter is moral peacocking, and every single Internet user's Caps Lock got stuck in the "on" position a few years ago, there's no shortage of finger pointing, moralizing, and heavy-fingered shaming.

The "free-range" parent and the "helicopter" parent are the ones most frequently at odds. The first believes children need freedom—and even danger—to grow and thrive. The second believes, probably due to astute observation, that little kids are morons in need of eternal help. Help from someone who can use a stove without burning down a house, or deploy toilet paper without just making the situation worse.

Utah recently approved a law that protects "free-range" parents from being charged with child endangerment or neglect. This means, when parents get hauled into court for not paying attention while their child climbed into the hippo pool at the zoo, they can employ the legal defense: "Yes, but I *meant* to not pay attention."

I've been accused of being both kinds of dad. Some people ask where my child is, see me ponder the question as if it were a vague philosophical inquiry, and assume I'm raising my four-year-old "free range."

"Where are any of us, really?" I might reply with a pensive look at the heavens.

Yet I often abandon this methodology, especially when I read about things like the kid who fell into a vat of crackling oil and was fried to death at a fast-food restaurant last year. Faced with those types of stories, I quickly putter over and hover for a bit, just to make sure the fruit of my loins doesn't put our primarily theoretical health insurance to the test.

The truth is, I have no idea how to raise someone who is both tough and gentle, both wise and trusting. I really don't.

People who say they do know are probably trying to sell you something, most likely a book about parenting, or perhaps the resplendent tail feather of a noisy moral peacock.

* * * * *

In the back of the Chauvet cave in France, those two ghosts walk eternally. Who knows what kind of parents that little prehistoric boy had. We know their brains were just as big as ours, but we have no idea how they saw and interpreted the world they inhabited. If modern humans today can't see through each other's eyes—imagine how differently a New York liberal and a rural Arkansas conservative see things— just think how differently those ancient people experienced life. Scientists suspect it was a place pervaded by magic, by nature, and by an intense fluidity between animal and human, male and female, alive and dead.

But I suspect parenting has always been parenting. We mammals, after all, are all defined by the way we raise our young. We're defined by our nagging doubts—I can almost hear Arg and Grr asking each other, "Do you think eight is too young to give a kid fire and let him explore a bear cave with his pet wolf?"—but also by our dreams. We are defined by our courage, our willingness to grab a torch and a long-toothed beast and venture out into the darkest corners of the world in search of adventure. And by the courage to let our children go out in search of adventure, at whatever age we finally decide to let them.

The way I see it, it's not a matter of which style of parenting is correct: helicopter or free-range. It's not really a matter of whether or not our kids can muster the intestinal fortitude to head out into the unknown.

Parenting, from the very moment you first lay eyes on your child, in a cave pervaded by the odor of bear dung, or in a hut, or in a hospital that smells of bleach, is merely a gradual summoning of faith—a slow stockpiling of bravery. You see and hold something small and fragile in your arms, and you can't imagine a world that will not shatter it. But somehow, most of the time, it doesn't break.

Our children grow, which is remarkable considering how much and how often they urinate and defecate, and the world does not break them. Then they grab a torch and head off into the endless caverns of this massive and glorious planet.

Eventually, if they don't get eaten by a cave hyena right away, you realize it's not their death you need to worry about. It's your own.

Then you understand you had it all backward. You finally recognize that you, too, are leaving footprints in the clay of this earth. And soon enough you will disappear, your torch flickering in the dark as you walk away, into the eternal haze of someone else's imagination.

YES!

*S*pree: The Big Magazine for Virile Men. *Flirt: The Magazine with the Velvet Touch. Midnight. Rapture.* Then there was *Blaze: Searing Excitement!*—a periodical that was basically calling itself *Chlamydia!* And of course, my personal favorite, the magazine for agreeable men with limited verbal skills, *Yes!*

The writers for these publications were so flamboyant and enthusiastic. I'd love to get my hands on one of their style guides, in which I'm sure the answer to any spelling inquiry, regardless of the word in question, was always "with an exclamation point!" They were mythological, comical, and epic, with splashes of color, flesh, and wordplay. At the heart of every story were women: Amazons, space travelers, and ancient Egyptian queens. They were part comic book, part classic literature, part gleeful nonsense. And part misogyny, of course.

I once took a college class in English literature. The teacher was an old poet who was crazy in the best possible way. He was a tall, lean, energetic man who delivered his lectures like sermons from a pulpit. He screamed, and laughed, and cried, and—this was my favorite—he sometimes whispered to us, beckoning us closer, glancing around in a clandestine manner, and spoke in hushed tones of the grand, ancient truths he had to impart. He said on multiple occasions that he dreamed of dropping dead—not taking ill, but definitively dying, complete with a biblical gasp and a hand to the chest—in front of the class one day.

When speaking of James Joyce, he paced up and down the aisles between students' desks, as if trying to whip us into an intellectual berserker frenzy. Sometimes he went one step further, and these little trips across the brown-carpeted floor brought him to unusual, often underutilized spaces in the room. Sometimes he finished his lecture perched, like a buzzard in a crooked necktie, in a third-story window frame, with one powerful, gnarled hand caressing the painted wooden frame above him, while the other rested on a knee that jutted up in front of his chest.

He said the key to successful parenting was a magical incantation. Every night, he explained, he had leaned over his infant son's crib and said: "You will be healthy, you will be successful, you will be happy." The rest of it—the diapers, the schooling, the vaccines, the feedings—were all just one big, trivial footnote to the vital spell cast at the center of his son's life.

When students questioned the spell's efficacy, he looked at them as if he'd been told the earth is flat. "It did work," he grunted. "He is."

He claimed to be ancient, like a member of one of those other species—the spirits of the sea or forest—and he looked it. But he apparently went on living for another decade after I left.

When, one day at work, sitting in a comfortable chair, I came across the news that he had died, I was saddened, not just by his passing, but also because there was no mention of it happening in front of an audience of horrified pupils. I read the full obituary, just in case, hoping to find some mention of the fact that counselors were being made available to help students deal with the shock. There was no mention at all.

As is often the case when I reflect on an obituary, I was surprised to learn the departed's life featured people other than me and times and places other than those in which I was present. He had a family, of course, and he went to the grave with a long list of academic accomplishments. But until I read that weird end-of-life list, he had existed, in my mind, only in the moments we shared together in that single, slightly dreary room full of people who were, for reasons I still don't fully comprehend, looking forward to careers in things like marketing and sports management. He won awards and created life, but I always assumed his greatest accomplishment over the course of 80-plus years was to impress and inspire a young man who, depending on at what time in the day the class took place, was either hungover or drunk.

* * * * *

In the back of the classroom sat a student different from the others. She was small and wrinkly, and her hair was short and white. Unlike the other students, she did not sunbathe on the lawn outside the main cluster of buildings on campus. I remember our professor treating her with extra care, perhaps because she was actually older than he was, or perhaps because she was the type of person you know you are supposed to admire.

She spent her youth as a woman in a time when women were often beaten with little or no consequence, and very few of them were encouraged to get a college degree. So she decided she would go back to school. It was admirable, which everyone knew from the moment they laid eyes on her.

Perhaps due to a limited, Social Security-based income, or because of essential frugality from living through the Great Depression, she saved money by purchasing an out-of-date edition of our textbook. While her anthology contained all the same poems and stories as the ones our parents had purchased for us, it was arranged differently, with different pagination and slightly antiquated footnotes and introductions. Even if she found the correct page, the paragraph in question would start or end in a different place on that page, adding another leg to her eternal journey toward the writings in question.

The class might as well have been taught in Klingon, for all she got out of it.

So, in addition to the inspired words of our brilliant professor, we could also look forward to an entire semester listening to the ample cacophony created by a confused but diligent octogenarian as she doggedly rifled through her textbook, occasionally stopping to read a passage she thought might have been what we were discussing—"Ah, no…"—and then resuming her eternal hunt for the place we all were. It was like watching a blind person trying to play *Where's Waldo?* It was depressing.

I remember hearing her, just as the professor released us from class one day and told us to have a good weekend, muttering to herself in bittersweet victory, "Here it is. I found it!"

If we had been characters in a movie, the woman's defining characteristic would have been some kind of undeniable majesty. We would have been in awe of her determination, her tenacity, and her spirit. We would have approached her after class, and we would have all become close friends, bridging the 60-year gap between us with the simple fact of our shared humanity.

Of course, that type of thing doesn't often happen in the real world, where she gathered up her useless pile of old books after each class and trundled off on fragile legs to exist in whatever distant, secluded realm she emerged from each Tuesday and Thursday.

So now, as I sit here, that is the end of her story. I never took the time to talk to her, so all I really know of her is that she was old, which—jokes aside—is not anyone's primary characteristic, because no one reaches old age without first being young.

* * * * *

That's not the case with Bonnie Logan. She's one of my favorite people. She is also a legendary pin-up model, or was, at least. Today, she's 83, probably about the same age my former classmate was. Splashed across the pages of a vast sea of mid-century magazines, with all their reds and yellows, sprawls this sensual, doe-eyed women with a come-hither look and life-raft-sized breasts. She is not merely beautiful or sensual; she is a spectacle unto herself, because to look at her is to imagine a story of adventure.

Writers for the publications in which she appeared— the ones so inordinately fond of sexy euphemisms—fawned over her, trying desperately to crank out phrases that could match her exotic visage. But God simply did not make enough exclamation points to write adequately about Bonnie Logan.

"She's cool as a Norse, warm as a gypsy, yet American as blueberry pie," raved one. Another said she was a "singer, swinger, model, and poet" who "made Hollywood her private playground." A different publication said she "ruled" the Floating Island Lounge where she sang. An L.A. newspaper, perhaps simply giving up at the end of the sentence, described her as "a singer, dancer, and eyeful."

A farm girl from a devout Midwestern family, Bonnie was a fierce individualist. "I never had to use the gun," she says of a Beretta she carried for protection. "Although I did have to threaten with it a couple times."

She's still a spectacle today, but one of a different kind. Several violent accidents and broken bones have left her hunched, and, I would imagine, in a great deal of chronic pain. She likes to claim a spot on the couch at the senior center, watching daytime television on the big-screen TV. But sometimes, when she flashes those eyes at you, you can still sense that inside her lives something epic. That she is a mythological creature—an Amazon, a space woman, and an Egyptian queen, all in one. That she is one of those other

species, a spirit of the sea or forest, and she is just imperson-
ating the ordinary humans.

"Sometimes I think things used to be better," she once
told me. "But then, old people always say that, don't they?"
Then she smiled. She smiles often when she talks about her
life, even though she had to make her way through sexism
and violence.

Our friendship started when someone gave me a tip
about a "little old lady" who lived across the street from a
dive bar. The type of person who feeds the neighborhood
cats and gets around, very slowly, with a walker and a great
deal of effort.

"She used to be a nude model or something," he said.
"That's what she says, at least."

When I finally tracked her down, which took some time
because she doesn't use computers or a reliable cell phone,
we agreed to meet for an interview at a little café. She
ordered a heaping platter of thick, fluffy pancakes, and cup
after cup of black coffee. She wore a long, puffy purple coat
that looked like a sleeping bag against the cold. On the back
of her chair, she hung a noisy plastic grocery bag. Out of it,
she pulled a fat, red scrapbook bound by a crimson ribbon.
As she laid it on the table and opened it, she said it
contained her life.

"This," she said, "is me."

For the next several hours, I sat with a tiny, elderly
woman and looked at topless photos of her as she told me
the stories behind each. In one, she pretends to garrote a
man. In another, she pinches a martini glass between two

exquisite fingers. She wears elegant gowns, cut-off blue-jean shorts with an unclasped bra, leopard-print lingerie, or nothing at all. There is something inherently biblical about the scenes.

Back then, she was a stunning manifestation of our species' capacity for beauty. She looked eternally young, with a broad, tapered face custom-designed to house her unique features. But of course, no one is eternally young. Not even her. And her visual beauty, however stunning, was only a launch pad for a sprawling story. We are a narrative species, after all. Giraffes have their long necks. Cheetahs have their speed. And we have the astonishing tales we live, imagine, and hear.

Years from now, when my daughter goes through her early childhood possessions, coated in a thick layer of dust and nostalgia, she will come across a glossy, black-and-white photograph of a beautiful woman with sultry eyes wearing a shimmering black dress. Perhaps it is not the most conventional gift for a daughter. A gift from Bonnie, a friend who lives life with an exclamation point, finding joy and beauty in an unfair world.

"For your daughter," she said as she handed it to me, smiling as the overhead lights glinted off the curvature of the image.

It will serve as a reminder, because someday my daughter will ask me if beauty is real. And I will reply, "Yes."

She'll ask if it's fleeting. Again, I'll say, "Yes."

I know what comes next, because the question is one we all ask when we are young.

"If everything is going to end someday, does any of it really matter?"

She'll look up at her dad, an agreeable man with limited verbal skills, and ask this question. I'll speak in a hushed tone, beckon her closer, and reply: "Yes!"

WINTER RAIN

When I woke up this morning, I meandered through the corridors of our home. It is pungent with our family odors—dogs and a cat and a child and a man and a woman—all sealed in as we await the end of winter. As the darker months progress, smells and detritus accumulate, waiting to be released in a ceremonial opening of windows and doors each spring.

I clutched a cup of coffee in my hand, its gentle warmth on my palm accentuated by staccato nips of direct heat on my tongue. I felt the liquid plunging down my throat, sluicing into my somnolent, troubled gut. I listened to the rain beating down and thought what a lovely sound it was. The patter and splash as each individual droplet of water was born, lived, then cried out in aquatic ecstasy at the exact moment it was smashed to bits by the earth at the end of its long, atmospheric tumble.

It was 5:15 a.m. Through the window I could just make out the snow-laden street through the blue light that gently segues the world from the black oblivion of night to the golden illumination of day.

"We don't get many rain storms in January, in Wisconsin," I thought, still somewhat languidly, as I wondered if 5:30 was too early to brew a second pot of coffee. "Especially when it's -3 degrees outside." Slowly, it dawned on me that any precipitation in the middle of winter should be arriving in the form of snow, not rain.

Then, like a character in a horror movie, a tingle ran down my spine: "It's coming from inside the house!"

I followed the noise, doing my best impression of a bipedal bloodhound in a bathrobe. It sounded less and less like a pleasant summer shower, and more and more like a rusty, shattered pipe spewing filthy, frigid water directly into our house.

"Please don't be sewage," I pleaded with a deity in whom I suddenly believed with the utmost conviction. "Please don't be sewage."

It was tricky for me, because I can only hear out of my left ear, which means I'm unable to triangulate noises. I can tell when music is playing, people are chattering, a fire engine is approaching, or water is being dumped onto the floor of my heavily mortgaged home, but I'm not good at figuring out exactly which direction the sound is coming from. I'm like the aural version of a cyclops.

The mystery solved itself when I opened a swollen door. I stepped through it into a different world. It was like Narnia, if Narnia were a room in a suburban house in which water had been leaking all night. Stepping into an icy puddle, I felt an instant, primal connection to the water. The cold liquid jolted and surrounded my feet. I wasn't merely on the water; I was in it. The experience would have been different if I had been wearing boots or shoes. I would have missed the experience of becoming one with the flood.

* * * * *

Being barefoot roots you to the world. Perhaps that's why it's so taboo. Because people constantly scurry to create distance and buffers between themselves and the planet that birthed them and will ultimately devour them. Like they and Earth are in a relationship, but after reading a pithy self-help book and speaking to a therapist, they've decided they need a little space. "I need some time to find myself," they tell the world.

I never realized just how strongly people feel about feet until I became friends, several years ago, with someone who refuses to wear shoes in public. To me, it seems like a very minor quirk. Like people who cut their hair in a ridiculous manner, which, here in the Midwest where grown men and toddlers favor the exact same fashion trends, is pretty standard. It's not nice to look at, but it's purely cosmetic, with no moral implications. But the extent to which my friend's barefootedness brings him into conflict with other people is astounding. Not a day goes by that he doesn't find himself kicked out of a building, denied service, or scolded and shamed for not covering his feet.

"It's against the law!" people shriek at him.

"It's disgusting!" yell others.

The first is demonstrably false. The second is undeniably true, but I'm not sure we should yell at people, or bar them from entering public buildings, just because we find parts of them unpleasant to look at. Maybe the next step would be to prohibit people with moles, or birthmarks, or eyes that aren't perfectly symmetrical from using our community centers. Should ugly people be allowed to use public libraries? Perhaps that's a question for another day.

Logically, it makes no sense. Feet, unlike shoes, are washed on a regular basis, so they spread far fewer germs than sneakers, sandals, and boots.

Yet bare feet are a big deal to people, all across the country. Many doors to businesses prohibit only two things: loaded firearms and visible toes. And unlike the prohibition on guns, the one on bare feet is nearly universal. In many Midwestern restaurants, you can actually dine with a loaded pistol on your hip, as long as you are wearing sneakers. Something about seeing someone's feet feels intimate and taboo. When someone sitting next to me on a park bench hoists a naked foot up onto his knee, I automatically look away, as if I didn't dare peer at something so personal. As if a big toe were actually a browser history, or an anus.

The only rationale is simply that people find feet displeasing to look at.

And they are, perhaps more so than any other body part. I, like everyone else I know, think my own feet are perfectly inoffensive. They are status quo feet. Everyone else's feet are grotesque. Every time I see a set of toes slightly different from my own, I have a strong visceral aversion. "Those don't look like mine," I think. "Those feet are incorrect." They're too short or too long, too narrow or too bulbous. The nails are too flat or too convex.

It's a bizarre reaction, and it's not one people have to any other body part. Show me someone else's face, or their hands, or even their genitals, and I won't immediately retch and feel disgusted that they don't look identical to mine. In fact, if any of those looked exactly like mine, I would be far more freaked out. With every other part of the body, we are far less bigoted. There is room in the world for all sorts of shoulders and hair, noses and legs.

When it comes to feet, we are universally intolerant. While it's not a huge problem by itself, I find it troubling that society as a whole can shun something simply because of the way it looks. I feel the same way about lawns, which are all required to look the same, and which, if they are populated by different plants and flowers and weeds, are believed to be signs of bad character.

* * * * *

There I stood, my feet bathed in the frigid waters at the bottom of an unintended indoor waterfall. The prior night had been a sleepless one. Our daughter had gone to bed with a fever, so I spent the darkest hours closing my eyes and trying to rest. Rather than counting sheep, I counted all the historical figures who had died of a fever. I'm a Russophile, so the list is pretty much infinite.

I tried to relax by reading a book, but when one of the novel's primary characters tragically perished due to a fever of her own, I decided it would be more relaxing to simply turn out the light, close my eyes, and harness the full powers of my imagination to envision all the ways our lives could go terribly wrong at any instant.

I didn't know it at the time, but as the hours passed, water was plunging into our house. While I imagined theoretical problems, I was blissfully unaware that I had a real one developing nearby.

Standing beneath my little waterfall, cold water bouncing off the ground all around me, I sipped hot coffee, the icy water on my feet, and realized today would be yet another series of small adventures. This time, I wouldn't even have to set out in search of them. This time, the adventures had come to me.

BEFUDDLE

Nothing brings edifying social interaction to a screeching halt as quickly as party games. They always makes me feel like someone who, on the verge of a spontaneous romantic encounter, sees his partner head to the hallway closet and return with a vast assortment of gear, complete with special chairs, whips, handcuffs, Viagra, and other aides.

"Shouldn't we at least try to do it ourselves first?" a reasonable person would respond. "I mean, shouldn't all these things be a last resort if we find out we can't get the job done on our own?"

I prefer authentic conversation. There are no written cues, no cards, no die, and no board determining what I can and cannot do or say. Aside from the general petty score-keeping we all do in our heads whenever we're in social situations, there should be no one allocating points.

These games come in many forms, but they tend to have names like *Befuddle* or *Incoherence*. They have subheadings that only confuse me further.

"The card game where you learn the mating calls of each state bird!" or "The board game where nouns are verbs, and adjectives are golden marmosets in estrus!" They are colorful affronts to the fact that we all have a limited amount of time on this planet.

Greta, my wife, says it's because I always lose, because I'm not acquainted with the sweet nectar of party-game victory. She is partially right. Most of these are games of chance, and while losing a contest of skill can certainly be disappointing, consistently losing games of chance is, philosophically at least, far more upsetting.

If I lose a 50-yard dash, I can at least acknowledge that my defeat was caused by a series of my own actions. But when I can't win at a game in which the champions are chosen exclusively by the gods of Fate and Chance, there is no silver lining. It's just affirmation of what I've long suspected, which is that the universe is conspiring against me.

The appearance of a party game usually coincides with a complete dismissal of all the usual rules of social etiquette. Then there is the emergence of disturbing, cliquish behavior.

"I know!" someone barfs during a lull in the conversation. "We should all play *Babble*. It's the game where saying what you don't mean is the key to victory!"

It's a grim turn of events. And I don't understand why doing this is okay, while standing up at the end of the meal and shouting "Let's all contract syphilis!" is not.

"That," I always say, politely but firmly, when someone suggests a party game, "sounds terrible."

When party games are involved, "no" suddenly stops meaning "no." To make matters worse, polite, soft-spoken people transform into terrible bullies whenever they catch the scent of a deck of silly trivia cards or a large board and dice.

"Come on, it will be fun!" they say, incorrectly.

"But it won't," I plead with earnestness to match their enthusiasm. "I'm not trying to be funny. It really won't."

"Okay, great, it's settled then," they reply, like they can't even hear me. "Matt will be on the blue team with Greta, I'll be the grand wizard, Brandon will speak entirely in Dutch, and Claire will put on the gorilla mask and roll the dice."

"I genuinely don't think this will be fun," I repeat. "I think it will ruin our night. And there isn't even anyone named Claire here right now..."

It feels like I'm having a stroke.

"Do you want to be the banker, the little train piece, or the number seven-and-a-half?"

Surely they serve a purpose, these games. But they were undoubtedly designed for people who don't genuinely enjoy each other's company. For people who don't have enough common interests to chat amongst themselves without a long list of instructions, written in a dozen different languages. It's as if they're trying to trick me into learning something.

Daily life is full of arbitrary rules. I see no need for them to diminish life's pleasantries and late-night conversations. When the party-game rules come out, I feel the same dread I felt when I unfolded the Dead Sea Scroll masquerading as the assembly instructions that came with our daughter's crib. "It says here I just need to attach this set screw to a hectare of headboard," I read, rubbing my temples.

There is no better way to simulate the experience of descending into madness than reading the rambling, incoherent instructions that accompany these insipid wastes of time. They are turbid at best and maddening at worst.

"It says here that everyone picks a card with a picture of a different type of camel on it," I read. "Okay. And whoever has been to Egypt most recently draws first, and single-humped dromedaries always beat two-humped bactrians. Then you write the first color that comes into your head on a scrap of paper, throw the paper away, and whoever writes 'red' on the back of their forehead first is the winner."

"I'm not sure I understand," I say. I'm hopeful my admission will prompt others to admit that they, too, don't understand the rules, or the pieces, or the cards, or the board. I'm always greeted with the blank stares of people who clearly think I'm either a smart person who is kidding, or a dumb person who is telling the truth.

My friends—I'll continue calling them "friends" here primarily as a matter of narrative convenience—chuckle condescendingly, the way you do when you have to explain to a two-year-old how to put on pants. Then they begin "explaining"—that's another word I'm using loosely—the rules to me. They try to verbalize the rules, they try to write the instructions down, and they try to act out a series of moves or a round in the game.

One such game, which I was forced to play on New Year's Eve last year, made literally no sense, was clearly dictated entirely by luck, and somehow I lost EVERY round. You had to look at a card with a picture on it, then say an unrelated word. Then everyone wrote down another, even more unrelated word, then they all compared what we had written, had a hearty laugh, and assigned zero points to me.

"The color nine!" said my friend's wife, Danielle.

"Good one. That's worth seven points! Matt, what did you write?"

"The letter orange?" I proffered, not without some hesitation.

"Ah, sorry. No. That's incorrect."

I have a friend named Ken. He's equally distraught.

I once saw "Fun Tuesdays" marked enthusiastically on a calendar on his refrigerator. I asked him what they were.

"My wife has her friends over every other week," he said. "They all make me play some kind of game—I think it's called *Cumberbunds and Cumberbunds* or something—where you draw a card and say a word, but not the word on the card. If you say the right word, you win."

"How do you know if it's the right word?" I asked.

He looked at me with a quiet, resigned desperation that will haunt me for the rest of my days. "I really have no idea, Matt. I just don't."

"And the worst part," he continued, glancing around the corner to make sure we were truly alone, "is all of them think I'm pretending I don't understand the game. You know, to be funny. But I really, truly don't know what's going on. I just don't."

"I hate..." he finished as he poured himself a stiff drink, "Fun Tuesdays."

We both agreed that if given a choice, we'd prefer Ebola Wednesdays or Botulism Fridays.

While over the years I've grown fairly adept at avoiding party games, I recently discovered a new scenario that includes many of the same elements: the personalized inscription at book signings.

"Make it out to *Willow from Stratford-upon-Avon*," someone says as she hands me a copy of my book and a modest line of people look on and wait. "Willow is with two "r's."

People mistakenly think that because I write books and newspaper articles, I must enjoy the physical act of writing. They assume I practice calligraphy in my spare time. Or watch spelling bees on television. But I compose my stories on a computer, and I frequently consult old-fashioned and digital reference books to find out if I'm "travelling" to a pub in England or "traveling" to a bar in the United States. My handwriting is shaky and erratic, making it look like my moods swing wildly from letter to letter.

I don't go to a painter's gallery and demand that she whip up a batch of Prussian blue in front of me, and I don't approach the chef at a local restaurant and ask him to milk a cow. Writing stories and writing inscriptions to someone's aunt are not exactly the same thing, and the skills required to do the former are not necessarily the same needed to do the latter. Book sales would indicate I haven't even figured out the former yet.

There are only two explanations for my poor performance in the realms of party games and personalized inscriptions. The first is that I'm mildly cognitively disabled. Perhaps just disabled enough that I haven't ever noticed it, and that I can't decipher simple game rules. Or, and my money's on this one, EVERYONE is equally confused ALL the time. The only difference between me and the rest of society is that, while I'm an idiot, they are idiots who are working overtime to conceal the fact. These are the types of people who furtively hide the seven extra nuts and bolts after assembling their new IKEA dresser, because they are mortified anyone might discover they didn't understand the directions.

Perhaps they are so used to being confused—and hiding it—that playing a board game in which the rules are open to wild speculation feels completely normal. After all, recent voting trends indicate most of the populace, when they are alone with their thoughts in a voting booth for 12 seconds, will simply have the electoral equivalent of a small seizure and walk out.

Not me. I don't know what the hell is going on. While it's not something I'm proud of—it's not like I'm from Florida or something—I am willing to admit it.

Maybe, just maybe, that means I'm winning.

THE NIGHT CHANG DIED

On the morning of January 17, 1874 Eng Bunker awoke to discover his conjoined twin, Chang, was dead. He couldn't leave the room to collect his thoughts. No covering the body with a sheet and heading downstairs to make coffee and weep. Eng had to lie there with death as an appendage, the granite weight of a mirror-image corpse preventing him from rising.

A few hours later, Eng died of what doctors at the time surmised was shock in the face of what even the most stoic person would find a pretty grim situation. Modern medical experts scoff at that explanation, saying he died of heart failure caused by a string of eleven Latin words. I can't help thinking that awakening eye-to-vacant-eye with the corpse of his twin might have played a teensy, tiny role in prompting his heart to stop.

There is a statue of these twins at a museum called Circus World in Baraboo, Wisconsin. There, inside a tent, stand plaster likenesses of people who used to appear in sideshows. A bearded lady. A very tall woman. A very small man. And the two men who, born near Bangkok, gave to the world the term "Siamese Twins." They married a pair of sisters who didn't get along, I learned, and they tried to live autonomous lives despite the fact that they were fused together by their cartilage and their livers.

The thought sometimes haunts me, arising like some two-headed Dickensian phantom while I lie awake at night.

To wake up and see your own death mask. It seems to me the one silver lining to dying is that you never have to deal with the aftermath. While your loved ones are left to cope with the grief and the mess, at least you are spared the shock of waking up dead. At least you don't have to open your eyes and see your face, identical but for the vanished spark of life for which science has no real explanation beyond the absurdly reductive, and which religion calls simply the soul.

These ghosts visit me at night. Visages of what was, or might have been, or might be or not be. I marvel at the way Dickens was able to put them into a story that captured the world's popular imagination during the day, because these spirits are nearly impossible to imagine out of context. Like dreams, they inhabit a turbid nighttime realm. In their natural habitat, they have form and meaning. Out of it, they are silly and absurd, like the dreams with which they cohabitate. Outside of the darkness, they quickly vanish.

When my three-year-old daughter wakes up from a nightmare, awash in panic and tears, her fear is palpable and real. Her flight from these demons is as real as anything. But the things from which she flees—polar bears, trolls, and Bengal tigers among them—are hardly threats in the small Midwestern town where we live. As she huddles in my arms, burrowing into me as if she wishes to magically conjoin and share some of her fear with me, she tells me in a blizzard of tears and mucus and descriptive terms about the terrors that pursue her.

"The monster was eating our house and we couldn't get away!"

Slowly, the gleam of day comes back into her eyes, she looks around, and she sees that the monsters have vanished. Sometimes she dreams that the things in her real life have turned on her. "The dog was trying to hurt me!" Then she looks down and sees the dog, who is nickering in his sleep, only harming us with an endless stream of toxic flatulence almost theological in its ability to shake our understanding of the world and our place in it.

Each morning, her ferocious beasts are gone. My dead doppelganger is gone. So are all the other ghosts that haunt us in the night. People frequently think of light as illuminating things. I think it's the opposite; I think what the light really does is hide things. It drops a golden veil over the ghosts and monsters who roam the earth with us. It doesn't harm them or vanquish them, but it does make them impossible to see, for a little while. And that's good, because they are distracting.

That must be why I awake each morning drunk on a feeling of almost limitless optimism. As the sun rises and I make coffee, I feel nothing short of euphoria. Waking up to find your conjoined twin turning blue next to you? What a preposterous thing to fret about!

So as dawn breaks, we venture out into the world, which is bright and solid. The ghosts of what was, or might have been, or might be or not be, are all obscured by the light. The world is ours alone. And together, like a ragtag band of post-apocalyptic wanderers—a little girl, a gastrointestinally troubled dog, and a man—we set forth to seek out new and exciting things.

AXE MAN

My pink, glittering wings flitted in the midday breeze as I hurled the axes.

Blade after blade bit into the wooden target. With every primordial "thunk," I felt my beard growing longer and my shoulders broadening. I was, for the first time in nearly 30 years, winning a competition that did not involve hunching over a desk and using my fingertips to tap daintily on little, chittering, plastic squares.

It started as a normal day. By the time the sun went down, I was a champion. Over the course of only a few hours, I went from a man who had never won any contest for throwing anything dangerous (a nobody, essentially) to a man who sank the blades of tomahawk after tomahawk deep into a round slab of wood.

Most of the people I defeated were weak children and drunk adults, but I didn't care. It happened at a festival in a crisp, bright clearing in the Wisconsin woods. The kind of place where everyone pretends they are visiting some bygone era.

The time and place can change. Some people set up camp at my friend's bison ranch, for instance, and pretend they are on the Lewis and Clark expedition. Others dress as knights and knaves and gently swing swords at one another. Still others set up permanent "historical villages," where people make cheese and shirts the hard way and explain to young, iPad-wielding school children that the median life expectancy used to be 13.

I was wearing jeans and a sweater. The modern kind—the kind made by a machine in a matter of seconds. The pink, bedazzled fairy wings that shimmered in the sun as I flung the ancient weapons at the target weren't meant for me. They were for my daughter. But she had abandoned them the way people discard things when their interest strays elsewhere. I carried the wings for a while, but it was easier to strap them to my back and liberate my hands for more important things like ale, axes, and my little girl.

As I threw, the target grew thick and cluttered with axe handles. There was little room in which to squeeze another one, even with my apparently deadly aim. So I embedded my next blade deep into the handle of one of the prior weapons, much like Robin Hood did when he split the arrow already embedded in the bullseye.

For the next few hours, I was a hero. My friends, unable to hide their admiration no matter how hard they tried, bought me beer and slapped me on the back.

"If the zombies come," observed one, "we know which useful skill you'll have."

I was like Beowulf, traveling from a distant land to slay a dreadful cookie of inanimate wood that had been terrorizing the local mead hall.

I would go home, I daydreamed, and purchase my own axes. I'd give them the names of beautiful women, know their every unique contour, and sleep with them under my pillow. Hopefully, if I got really lucky, one night a man—or a massive troll, would break into my house, lumbering up the stairs in search of treasure to abscond with, and people to murder along the way. As he turned to creep down the black, narrow, photo-lined hallway that leads to the place where my family sleeps, I would emerge from my bedroom, hairy and grunting, as if I were slipping out of a portal from another time. The intruder, his heart gripped by fear, would raise his gun and level it at me from the other end of the hall.

"You," I'd utter, "just brought a gun to an axe fight."

In the dark void he would somehow be able to hear my mouth stretching into a grin as I spoke. With that I would hurl one. He would hear its faint, melodious whistle, growing louder and more rapid as it raced toward his skull. In his confusion, he'd forget to fire his weapon, until— "Thunk!"—it was too late.

He would fall, and I would put my foot on his chest, yanking out my weapon like a young King Arthur. Depending which iteration of the dream I was having, I would either call the police (if he was human) or hack off his head and mount it on my wall (if he was a troll).

Over the following weeks and months, I started watching more and more online videos of people making, throwing, and even (this is where it gets a little embarrassing) just talking about axes. I ordered a few inexpensive ones, and set up a target—a rustic, three-legged easel on which a round slab of wood sits—in the backyard. After a few months, the thrill I got from throwing those axes started to soften. Better axes existed, I knew, and I needed them.

For my birthday, I ordered myself a Medieval French throwing axe, which has a point that tapers up and helps it stick when it hits wood (these days) or craniums (in the Middle Ages). I also ordered a "bearded" Viking axe. It's a meticulous recreation of one found, stashed amid a horde of monastery gold and jewels, in what is now Gotland, Sweden.

Axes say so much about the people who wielded them. Some were used primarily for building ships, or making fence posts to contain sheep whose brains would later be eaten by people. Others had special features designed specifically for the warrior who really wanted to shatter the skulls of children and the infirm.

I now know the whole axe lexicon, too. I get so immersed in axe lore online that sometimes, when my wife walks in the room, I jump a little as her presence pulls me back into modernity. I blush and snap the laptop closed.

"I'm just looking at pictures of a French lady," I assure her. "I started by looking for images of a Norwegian one with a big beard, but then I kind of got sucked in. You know how it goes." She knows that "lady" is a term for a light throwing tomahawk, and I'm fairly certain she knows that some axes have beards.

She has not left me yet.

* * * * *

As the festival wound down on the day I fell in love with axes, perspective returned. I bested most of the competitors. Many had been pre-pubescent, and they clearly weren't taking the competition as seriously as I was. But for a few hours that day, it felt like I lived in another time, and I felt like the hero of some Viking saga, even though I don't and I'm not.

Yet the question remained: From whence did my impressive strength and stamina spring?

Modernity is an interesting place to live. But there is nothing particularly special about it. After all, everyone who has ever lived, lived in what were then considered "modern" times. No one ever walked out of their mud hut or cave or castle one fine morning, stretched their arms out wide and exclaimed, "It's good to live in the past!"

The future, when it gets here, is never quite as sleek as we expected it to be. Yet the time we live in right now is always dynamic. It is already the present, it was recently the future, and it will soon be the past. It is a time in which I sometimes win axe-throwing competitions.

＊ ＊ ＊ ＊ ＊

As I left the fair with my prize that day, I picked up my daughter and effortlessly tossed her high into the air and onto my shoulders. There she sat, perched above the petite wings of a bulky man who is good at throwing axes. While I lifted her from the ground, I suddenly realized why my arm was so strong in the first place.

It was her.

It was all the times I had lifted her up to give her a hug or a ride, or to prevent her from setting one of our pets on fire. I have the fabled dad strength, and that's why I'm so good at throwing axes.

Just then, some nerd who knew a little bit about physics, but absolutely nothing about parenting, sized me up. "Look at the size of those wings compared to his body," he commented to a friend who fell in stride beside him. "I seriously doubt he's going to fly away anytime soon."

My daughter balanced atop my shoulders and looked out across the clearing in the woods. It was drenched in the rich highlights of late-afternoon sun as people streamed toward the parking lot. I clutched her ankles firmly in my hands.

I wondered if the stranger had any idea just how wrong he was.

BORING DEATH

You can envision the dearly departed on the verge of death, clutching a loved one's hand as the light inside starts to flicker, wheezing: "Please, when you select my headstone, make sure it's…unremarkable."

Graveyards in the American Midwest are missed opportunities. The neatly mowed rows of economical, hardy, unpretentious markers. To walk through a graveyard in Wisconsin is to see 300 dead people trying desperately not to outdo one another, the types of people who, when asked to "pick a number," will invariably go with "6," because that's surely enough. Anything more, to a practical Midwesterner, seems greedy, presumptuous, or just plain wasteful.

I've been to other parts of the country. I've even lived in some of them, including, somewhat regrettably, Florida, where the swampy ground makes traditional burials a mucky, challenging endeavor. When you try to give people there a decent burial, the earth tends to spit them back out, essentially saying: "No thanks." But at least in the swampy southern hinterlands, graveyards are beautiful, mossy, and pleasantly ostentatious. Like little jungle gardens where stone mausoleums and statues of angels and saints grow crookedly out of soggy soil and slowly disintegrating human lives.

In Wisconsin, humility is just embedded in people's DNA. Expecting them to be resplendent in death is like asking them to come back as zombies and open up a financially viable minotaur farm.

There is a place called the Dickyville Grotto. It looks like any old Catholic shrine, dedicated to God and country, with the notable exception that every square inch is festooned with things like petrified sea urchins and fool's gold. It's wonderful, largely because visitors leave knowing exactly what it would look like if Saint Francis and the sea god Poseidon had been involved in a violent head-on collision. It's not actually a graveyard, though, since there are no dead bodies rotting just beneath your feet when you walk the grounds.

I've always wanted to be shot out of a cannon, or tied to the mast of a ship before the sails are set on fire with burning arrows, when I die. "That way people will remember me!" I think, briefly forgetting that I will probably feel little or no vindication when that day actually comes.

Worried my life will not be worthy of note, I skip ahead and plan a death that I think people could get excited about. So, maybe these practical Midwesterners have boring graveyards because they're generally happy with their body of work while alive. Maybe they aren't worried they will be forgotten, because, along with frugality, an inability to get a haircut not from the 1930s, and the almost pathological compulsion to fry cheese, they know they've made a mark, in the people they were kind to, or the ones they nourished and nurtured.

Maybe I won't need to be shot out of a cannon when I die. Maybe my life will be enough.

Or, and I'm fairly certain this is correct, the best option is to live the way Midwesterners do. To be kind and measured. When life does end, the time to start acting like an ancient, egomaniacal Babylonian king will finally be at hand.

In death, I can have an enormous, colorful monument built to celebrate my plainspoken, practical approach to life, and my incredible, towering modesty. Then I can have that monument slathered in luminescent pink, covered in seashells, and shot out of a cannon, high into the heavens. It will be a bold, italicized, underlined exclamation point on the end of a solid, sensible story.

CHICKENS OF THE APOCALYPSE

I'm not a doomsday prepper. Such people, who you've probably witnessed on one of those reality TV shows that tend to exploit individuals with mental illness, are far too eager to see bloodshed and human suffering just for a chance to drink their own purified urine and say, "I told you so."

But on some mornings, when the arctic snows have frozen the world and silenced all of humanity, I trundle outside to be with the chickens. As they hum their scratchy songs against a backdrop of quietude, I like to fantasize that everyone is dead.

Not everyone, of course. I'm still here, obviously, and so are the chickens. My wife is still around, and so is my daughter. The people I love most, whose lives give my life meaning, have been miraculously spared. But the people who spend all their time treating their fellow human beings as a 24/7 grievance department, lamenting the fact they must wallow through another day of existence on this particular planet, they're all gone. The people who couldn't find happiness unless everything was just right—they all fell victim to the great plague.

I recently greeted a stranger with my best "How's it going?" at a birthday party for someone else's kid and was immediately treated to a very long, very passionate, ennui-filled diatribe about the state of the world. The stranger wove through topics ranging from poverty and hunger to gerrymandering and fossil fuels. It wasn't really the type of thing I want to listen to while eating cake with shiny red letters written in perfect gelatin-flavored script. But after the apocalypse, I can finally eat my cake in peace, assuming people are still eating cake once civilization has collapsed. While I wait for the end of the world, I can at least complain about the complainers, which is at least a complaint of the meta variety.

Our chickens live in a red and yellow house behind our garage. An unstable pile of wood doubles as a fence, shielding us from any prying eyes on that side of the property. Rather than dither with the pile, I intend to build a shed around it. It's on my to-do list.

My very long to-do list.

Sometimes the chronically unhappy become ideological zombies, with their own brand of menace, but lacking the verbal skills to inundate the rest of us with coherent complaints. Instead, they speak in a deep guttural murmur I don't understand. Not like the hens, which somehow make themselves useful without having to be witty or self-aware.

Some of the hens are covered in black and gray bands. Others are the room-temperature orange of a well-worn basketball. One looks like Pablo Picasso used her as a canvas. All of them illustrate that intelligence, beauty, and utility do not run in tandem. They're pleasing to me in this post-apocalyptic setting, where you have to watch out for roving gangs—but at least no one is around to misunderstand a rhetorical greeting.

My desire for a post-apocalyptic world is mostly aesthetic. And the chickens, along with the general detritus that makes up my yard, fit nicely into the genre. Because when small bands of people struggle onward after our phones and computers all stop working, you just know we'll need plenty of protein to eat, lots of compost to use on our fields, and a way to dispose of food scraps before the rats and undead possums get to them.

We've had chickens for years. Their lives are small and filled with little or no intellectual discourse. But they are lives, with all the ontological connotations that entails. We once had a chicken that was shiny azure, with a fluffy neck beard like the one worn by Henry David Thoreau. Another had feathers that looked like marmalade slathered onto white scales, with a fluffy, ostentatious crown of feathers on her head. The crown completely covered her eyes and looked like it had been designed by a loopy shaman. She refused to sleep in the coop with the others, until I found her one frigid winter morning, decapitated, lying stuck and partially submerged in a little frozen pond of blood in a yard of pristine white snow.

Her head was completely missing, which likely had little impact on her IQ but did deprive her of her primary attribute, which was a bizarre, simple-minded grandeur. With her body hard and her wings dramatically spread, she looked like the victim of some ancient pagan sacrifice.

When I picked her up, I realized she had ceased to be what a living body is. She was no longer a system of different parts working together. United by cold death, she was merely one frozen item, hard but shockingly light without the heft of life burning inside her. Two mornings later, I found another chicken—this one big and white and significantly less ornamental—in the same pose. Her head was also missing. A weasel, or a witch doctor, or possibly a weasel witch doctor, was clearly on the loose in our neighborhood. Out came a shiny new lock for the coop.

I'd been aware that people who display cowardice are often called "chickens." What I hadn't realized until that moment was that, like the hemophiliac, chickens have every reason to be nervous. Their skittishness is not paranoia. It's legitimate fear. There are very few things that can't kill a chicken, really. Yet in other ways, these animals are surprisingly tough. In fact, when they sport their adult feathers, even the most frigid temperatures won't bother chickens. This is useful during the long nuclear winter.

Having grown up on a farm, I know death. I also know manure. Farm kids like me spend most of their formative years shoveling, raking or pitchforking dung—sometimes in the shape of pancakes, sometimes of nuggets, sometimes of pellets—out of various stalls and paddocks. Individuals who didn't grow up in an agricultural setting have a difficult time wrapping their suburban minds around this concept.

My wife loves animals, but every time we bring home a new pet, there's an awkward moment when the creature reminds her, in the most visceral way possible, of this one truism. Her countenance will grow dark. She'll look at the droppings with alarm: "It's going to the bathroom! Right there!" She's amazed in a different way, but to very much the same degree she would be if the animal suddenly announced, in the voice of David Attenborough, that it had figured out how to travel through time.

Cats go about their business with so much secrecy it might as well be a drug deal. For dogs, it's not such a clandestine affair, but they at least have the decency to look embarrassed while doing it, and I've always considered shame to be a sign of first-rate intelligence.

Not chickens. They don't even stop eating, drinking, or walking. But this too is a blessing since their waste can be turned into compost, which we can use to grow life-sustaining crops once all the convenience stores burn to the ground during the terrible, terrible event.

The chickens' hierarchical aviary society is fun to watch, which will come in handy when we no longer have television. One day, when I reached into the coop to retrieve some eggs, one of them scuttled out from beneath my hand. It wasn't an egg; it was a rodent. It was below zero outside, and out of the pinewood shavings burst a huge rat, his pink tail dragging through the chicken droppings as he disappeared into a few feet of old snow. When I looked it up online, I discovered that there are no wild white rats, which means the one who tried to make a nest in my chicken coop had been a little girl's pet.

"Where did Cecil go?" I imagined the kid down the street asking her mom.

"Well, Jezebel," her mother would reply, "you left the top of his cage open last week and now he's getting hypothermia in the neighbor's backyard while he listens to the sounds of a grown man screaming."

Maybe the rat made his way back home and was reunited with his owner. Maybe the weasel captured him and gnawed off his head. Maybe he made it as far as the pine tree on the far side of the chicken pen, then turned into a freeze-dried mummy like that human Iceman, Ötzi.

Sometimes I take a break from looking forward to the apocalypse. Sometimes I look back into the befuddling mist of my childhood. I hated growing up on a farm, feeling I was being punished for some unknown crime because I didn't live on a busy street and get all my food from a supermarket.

Now, though, when I slip outside just before sunrise each morning to let the chickens out, I feel like a farm kid again. Except this time I'm old enough to appreciate it. When I do the little chores that chickens require, I feel like a slightly fatter, wiser version of the child who did these same things with chickens, cows, and horses all those years ago. A smart, resourceful, happy man who is doing a good job fending for himself and his family in a strange, imperfect, and often troubling world.

There's a certain peace to it. The world is already broken. Of course it is. We've lost many of the people and ideas we once loved. But here we are, alive and happy as we head into the future.

FLOYD

always loved hurricanes, even before one of them made
me famous.

As a kid in New England, they were like holidays. They
battered homes and storefronts, and families turned to
indoor camping, gathering near the extra batteries, canned
goods, candles, and—my favorite—board games.

I used to imagine that once it was all over with, once
the final storm cells had uneventfully passed, we'd emerge
from our family cave as the lone survivors of an uncertain
plague. My dad was camp leader and my little sister was the
proverbial canary in the coal mine, reporting back to us what
was happening outside.

Then I grew up and headed to northern Florida. A few
weeks after I moved into my college dorm, I stepped onto
the balcony of my new cave and it appeared to me that
everybody in the city was going camping, outdoor camping
—everyone except me.

Squinting down, I saw cars packed like explosives with
backpacks and food, streaming out of the dormitory's
parking lot. My old friend, confusion, suggested that I find
out what was going on.

Heading downstairs to the common area (I didn't have
a television), I saw a small group of people huddled around
the TV, their eyes wide as Wile E. Coyote's upon realizing
he's too far from the cliff to make it back. On the television,

a radar image showed a menacing rainbow of colors moving not only toward the Sunshine State, but me.

The hurricane looked about the size of Russia. Its name was Floyd and, according to the National Hurricane Center report, it was a killer. The zipper of text scrolling along the bottom of the screen displayed only one word: *Evacuate!*

I strolled back to my dorm in the awkward manner of someone trying to stay cool under great emotional duress. In the few minutes I'd been gone, my roommate, who I suddenly suspected was The Flash or maybe some kind of warlock, had gathered all his belongings and fled.

The storm was troubling, yes, but so was the fact that, with all my roommate's stuff gone, I realized I didn't own many things. I didn't have shampoo, socks, or a pillow. I didn't even have any batteries, much less a radio to put them in. I did not have a car, or even a bicycle. Neither had seemed vital when I planned my move to St. Augustine.

"It's Florida," I had thought to myself with a shrug. "Getting around will literally be a walk on the beach."

I hadn't envisioned a scenario in which I was forced to flee on foot from an angry sea. My nearest relatives lived in Massachusetts, and I had focused all my energy during my first few weeks in college on aggravating my professors, rather than making friends my own age.

I tossed things around in my room, primarily beer funnels and music CDs mixed in with the odd textbook, looking for something useful. The best I could come up with was an unyielding old bagel and a half-eaten jar of creamy peanut butter. I hadn't purchased either of them, but

I felt comfortable claiming them in light of the dire situation.

Our school, once a hotel for the wealthy, was gorgeous —an ocher and white assortment of Spanish-influenced spires and terraces, dappled with verdant palm trees. My dorm, on the other hand, was drab and dismal. I wasn't keen on hanging out there on bright, sunny days while I was alive. I certainly didn't want it to become my tomb, despite the fact that it already looked very specifically like one.

Unsure what to do, I dragged a cooler full of bargain beer down to the nearly empty parking lot. Perched atop it, I pondered my next move carefully, like a champion chess player whose king is perilously close to running out of places to hide.

A shaggy-haired surfer, wearing a Boston Red Sox cap, a blue-and-white tank-top and flip-flops that made him sound like a horse trotting on cobblestones, jogged across the lot. He was followed by a ragtag mob of what appeared to be groggy refugees.

I looked more closely and recognized something: they were people like me. Each carrying one or two items and nothing else. One guy simply had a collapsible lawn chair.

As they piled into a rusty Volkswagen bus, someone I recognized from English Literature 101 stuck his head out.

"Mike, right?"

I nodded. Sure. Why not? Mike was a perfectly good post-apocalyptic name.

"Get in!"

I stood up and started walking toward the vehicle, but was quickly turned back by much hand waving and yelling.

"Bring that!" they yelled in the pitch-perfect unison of a well-trained choir, pointing at the bulky cooler.

We made our way inland for the next 12 hours. So did nearly every resident of coastal Florida, which significantly slowed our pace.

We spent most of our time idling or driving at a leisurely pace of about 15 miles per hour. The decrepit bus overheated when not in motion, so we were eventually forced to turn the engine off during lengthy stops on the highway. Eventually, fearing we might run out of gasoline and be stranded on the side of the Florida interstate—a place that is decidedly the domain of serial killers, rogue alligators, and insects bigger than both of them—we decided to simply push the van on the downhill stretches.

Crashing on the floor of a cigarette-scented Tallahassee motel room that night, I chatted with my fellow travelers and gazed up at a little TV screen. On it, a cable news program was recapping the desperate evacuation attempts of Florida's very weird population.

"As you can see," the newscaster said with palpable excitement, "people are doing whatever it takes to get out of the storm's path."

On the fuzzy TV screen, an overhead image popped into view. Taken from a helicopter, it showed a motley assortment of young men, wearing flip-flops, shorts, and sunburns. They were pushing a rusty van down a gridlocked stretch of highway. They were clearly quite drunk.

It looked like the beginning to a pretty decent movie in which there would be very few survivors.

"It's…" stuttered a voice from somewhere else in the motel room. "It's us!"

There were 57 deaths directly attributed to Hurricane Floyd. Most, according to the National Hurricane Center, were due to drowning in freshwater flooding. Floyd was the deadliest hurricane in the United States since Agnes in 1972, causing $1.325 billion in damage.

I was spared. Since I didn't really own anything, it didn't even cost me much. And it made me famous, even if only a small handful of guys in a putrid motel room knew it.

THIS WAS WRITTEN
BY A NEANDERTHAL

"I was more destitute than the cave dweller; but then the memory—not yet of the place in which I was, but of various other places where I had lived and might now very possibly be—would come like a rope let down from heaven to draw me up out of the abyss of not-being…"
—Marcel Proust

etecting the blood of Englishmen used to be the work of cranky giants who lived atop stalks that sprouted from magic beans.

My, how the world has changed.

These days, all you have to do is spit into a vial and mail it to a group of scientists. They cracked the human genome, and they can look at your DNA and tell you why you are bald, or too short to go on carnival rides, or allergic to coffee.

Some genetic secrets, when you unlock them, when you learn them, seem very much like grim medical diagnoses. Others, a stroke of fate. Who knows how many siblings I would have had were it not for the lethal recessives they inherited from one parent or another. Others feel like the modern equivalent of a "yo mama" joke. As in, you got so much Neanderthal DNA, yo mama is basically a sasquatch.

If you want to know how many Neanderthal genes I have, the answer is probably "more than you." More than 84 percent of the people tested actually, and the sample size was international and enormous. I have 302 genetic variants that can be traced back directly to those cave dwellers. We cave people are notoriously bad with numbers, but even I can tell that's a lot.

The news surprised me. Perhaps it was less of a shock to the many girlfriends, schoolteachers, and literary critics who, despite no laboratory or advanced understanding of genetics, have been implying it for years. It certainly explained why I like cave paintings so much.

Before my stout, heavy-browed ancestors died out, they interbred with my *Homo sapiens* ancestors, hence the evidence of them in the DNA in my spittle. Most non-Africans today have some Neanderthal DNA. Most sub-Saharan Africans have little, or none. I, apparently, have a lot—about four percent of my total DNA.

We've all seen those genealogy commercials with the spouse who thought she married an Italian, only to discover through a DNA test that he's actually a wombat. I took the test in part because I wanted that type of surprise, and because, like so many people, I crave identity.

For many years prior to my genetic test, I was under the impression that I came from Vikings. With bone beads dangling in their beards as they stood in the prow of a dragon-led longboat, hands clutching heavy axes, crashing, falling, and rising on their way through a salty ocean mist, they embarked on conquest and adventure. They filed their teeth to little, bloody stumps, a painful process that drastically shortened their lives, for no other reason than to terrify their enemies with the knowledge that they were willing to drastically shorten their lives for no good reason.

"If I'm willing to do this to myself, just imagine what I'll do to you," those bloody teeth grinned at their enemies.

Even their gods were cool. They had names like Odin and Thor, and they loved to fight, drink, and party. I knew they weren't my only ancestors, but I live in the Midwest, a part of the country where people love to draw lines back to those adventurers.

They came up with the best names. Names like "Skull Splitter," "Fork Beard," and "Blood Axe." One of their leaders was called "Ivar the Boneless," which some people think refers to missing limbs, others think means he had a rare genetic disorder, and some scholars think means he was both impotent and a braggart, which I think is a very original combination.

Vikings were crazy and wild, and they were my great-great-grandparents many times over.

Except they aren't. Not to any spectacular degree, at least.

My DNA revealed I'm only 14 percent Scandinavian. Most of my ancestors are genetically English and Irish. That means they were the ones being raided by Vikings, not the ones doing the raiding. It means most of my ancestors weren't standing in the prow of a boat, crashing through stormy seas, with blood dripping from their teeth. No, most of my ancestors were harvesting wheat in their little villages, praying the furious men of the North would not cleave them in twain and take all seven of their earthly possessions.

Then, at some point, their vastly different cultures came together. Some invaders stayed and settled and farmed. People—people who had been sworn enemies—loved each other, and they had children together.

Today, for all our fancy, genome-cracking scientists and our explosion of knowledge and progress, we can't even get people with slightly different political beliefs into the same room with one another. Conservatives can't tolerate people who don't believe in the exact same version of the Christian God they do. Liberals brag about how outraged they are by everything that exists outside the margins of their narrow worldview, accusing anyone without an identical philosophy of being a bigot, and somehow doing it without a hint of irony.

These days, a Methodist and a Lutheran being civil to one another feels like real progress. And they are reading from the same Bible, in the same language, about the same God, while wearing the same clothes and eating the same food.

A thousand years ago, an oxherd or cheesemaker who believed in Jesus fell in love with a raider who believed in Thor and Odin. They both smelled terrible, spoke different languages, wore different clothes, and yet somehow they settled down together, living, laughing, eating, and drinking under the same roof. He would kneel down in a Christian church, and she would look on and think, "Oh, so this is where you go to take refuge from death and oblivion." He would see her clutching a figure of Freya on her sleigh pulled by cats, and think the same thing. In the blink of an eye, mortal enemies became friends. Their children became adventurers and emigrants, and they encountered other, equally foreign gods and people. How else do you explain the smattering of East Asian and Ashkenazi Jewish DNA in my saliva?

My DNA unlocked even more secrets. Through my mother's "haplogroup," which means something sciency, I suspect, it traced me back to a single woman who lived some 11,000 years ago. Her ancestors migrated into Europe from the Middle East as the Ice Age receded. Her children's children's children eventually ended up in a field in Britain, drinking ale for breakfast and hoping not to see dragon-studded ships rising out of the sea that day. Their descendants would eventually board different ships and head west, to a New World.

And now, here I am today, living in the middle of that New World as it slowly reaches middle age.

Going back some 40,000 years, in ways that are both literal and allegorical, I'm the baby of a Neanderthal and a modern human, who came together through what was surely a mixture of brutality, pure chance—and hopefully love.

After all, that's how we all live, and that's how DNA mingles. A man and a woman joined together to produce offspring, and in addition to having different gods, different languages, and different bone structures, they probably weren't even the same species. Yet once again, being together, being loved and sharing shelter, food, stories, and DNA, was far more important than their many stark differences. They only had a few things in common, but one of them was the capacity to love, and that mattered more than everything else.

This Neanderthal DNA adds an almost infinite prologue to my story. And stories, even more than flesh and blood, are what we are all made of.

It's exciting, surprising, and terrifying with splashes of beauty and splendor at just the right moments. Anyone who tells you we're all the same is selling something. Anyone who claims that 7 billion people, with all their different foods, gods, rituals, genders, sexualities, races and languages, are all "the same" is making a comically dangerous oversimplification.

We are not all the same. We're not even all equal. Some have power, some have health, some have poverty and disease. Some are right, and some are wrong. But we come together, again and again, despite—even because of—our many differences.

As a Neanderthal living in a world of modern humans, I sometimes get the urge to take refuge from the swirling madness around me. I want to run off and hide in a dark, quiet cave somewhere. If I did, I'd probably mash up some berries and start telling a story on the rocky wall there. A story about the many kinds of people who have so few things in common yet can't stop having babies together. When it was done, I would look at it and see a love story. Then I would grunt, smile, and lumber off to search for food.

THE RIVER

The portrait would be massive. Too big for mortal eyes to consume in a single glance. The oil paints would be thick, rich, and dark, full of ridges and valleys, like a stormy green sea frozen in time and slathered on canvas. In it, I would sit in a tall, wooden chair, with the hide of a wild beast, the scents and spirits of the deep forest still trapped within its fibers, draped over the back.

On my left would sit a massive white hound, its ears cropped into horn-like points, its chest deep, its carriage noble. On my right, its twin would slumber, soaking up the crackling heat from a nearby fireplace, over which a black, cast-iron cauldron would gurgle and steam. The dogs would sleep in shifts, one at a time, I thought. Always, one would be vigilant and watchful. Always, one of them would scan the horizon for something to hunt or fend off. Both would have an assortment of healed scars from the thrusts of various yellow-tusked boars.

I would sit in my chair, my lips stained by a trace of ruby-red wine. Wine from my cellar, I thought, which was just down the spiral staircase. If you reach the dungeon and hear the moans of my enemies, you've gone too far. On my lap, a crossbow, as proof of my capacity for violence. On a stand next to me, an assortment of books about love and philosophy—a reminder that my eternal quest for knowledge would always temper my mighty violence with the resplendent light of justice. The color of evening moss would abound, as would the burgundy of animal life.

My partially devoured dinner would sit nearby. Perhaps sustainably roasted flamingo, or grilled haunch of giraffe. Something exotic yet responsible.

My beard dark. My brow heavy. My eyes an intense walnut brown. I would smell, you would imagine, like a bear wearing a trace of pleasant, exotic oil.

"Should there be a dragon's head on the wall?" asked Ken.

I shook my head. "No, no, I want this to be realistic. If it's not realistic, the whole thing will never work."

"Maybe a troll's head, then?" he interjected.

"Well, maybe…"

We were sitting in the living room of a house the exact size and shape of a trailer, on top of a couch that was more stain than fabric. We were hunched forward, doodling and writing over a coffee table that was more stain than wood. If we were going to convince my ex-girlfriend to take me back, this painting had to be just right. It had to show her what the man she had given up could look like, and what he could be, if only she would allow him to continue residing in her New Jersey apartment, where he could live off of care packages sent by her parents, work part-time at a nearby shopping mall, and think good and hard, for five or six years, about what to do with his life.

We'd parted ways, after five years together, over the phone. I was standing at a payphone outside a convenience store in Florida. Just inside the door was a stack of newspapers featuring one of my very first bylines. The story was fluffy and the pay was $20, but seeing my name in print gave me a real thrill. I suggested we break up, primarily just to get my girlfriend's attention, and she called my bluff with a casual tone that nearly made me cry.

"Sure," she said. "Why not? I'll talk to you again sometime, or maybe not."

I hung up and drove my white, mold-infested, Petri dish of a car away, putting my foot to the floor and reaching 70 miles per hour, a speed I maintained until I killed the engine back at my trailer. I've never been a fan of driving fast or recklessly, so the speed wasn't an expression of my emotional state. The car's radiator was cracked, and the only way to keep it from overheating—and eventually blowing up, I worried—was to drive like a bat out of hell, allowing the wind to power the fan, which kept the engine from glowing red and turning molten.

I would have driven the same way were I fleeing a horde of cannibalistic, shotgun-wielding swamp people riding on the backs of genetically modified panthers—a regular sight in Florida back in those days—or driving to the store for a pint of ice cream. Hell, I would have driven just as fast on the way to my own lobotomy. It was the only way to get anywhere without the car breaking down.

I licked my figurative emotional wounds by literally drinking a gallon jug of concord grape wine. I briefly dated a woman who was equal parts human being and tornado of perfume, hair dye, makeup, and leopard-print shawls. I was terrified of her, and of her father, and of her mother, all of whom, I assumed, were heavily armed at all times.

One day, I told her I needed to fly home to Massachusetts for the weekend. Would she give me a ride to the airport in Jacksonville, please? Sure, she said, watching as I packed every single thing I owned into two suitcases and one olive-green backpack.

The car I left under a bridge, with the keys in it. The license plates I flung into a garbage bin.

We chatted on the way to the airport. Inside, we exchanged a lengthy hug during which I was reminded, one last time, of her incredible physical strength. I passed through the metal detector and my backpack passed through the X-ray tunnel. With an army of security personnel, a long line of passengers, and several barriers and warning signs between us, I finally felt my courage growing.

"I think we should break up!" I called to her as she waved goodbye. "I'm sorry."

Only a year had elapsed since a group of terrorists had flown airplanes into the Twin Towers in New York. Security was incredibly tight. There was nothing she could do but lower her hand and look upset, but once again much less upset than I like to think a woman should be to see me walk out of her life forever.

It was a few weeks later when Ken and I dreamed up the painting. We drank inexpensive beer, which thrived on a marketing campaign that bragged about its coldness rather than its taste or quality of ingredients, and tried to think of ways to get Sara, whom I had last spoken to on a payphone outside a convenience store in Florida, to take me back. The painting of me with the hounds was our best idea yet. Ken's interest was based partially in altruism, but primarily, he made it quite clear that I couldn't sleep on his couch forever. Sometime soon, the day would arrive when I would have to peel myself off that bed of stains and go somewhere else.

Ken was so genuinely nice. His face round, affable, and dotted with freckles. His hair, which he styled by putting on a tight stocking cap immediately after showering, was round and black, and his heart was kind, if slightly overwrought by his diet and lifestyle.

Sara has seen me at my worst many times. She had seen me and my dog eating frozen hamburgers and canned mixed vegetables night after night. She had seen me burgled time and time again. And she had seen me wander through life waiting, always waiting, for something to happen—waiting for the perfect circumstances in which I could prove my worth and thrive. As a writer. As a philosopher. As a man. As a moral actor.

She waited for me to stop waiting, and I waited a little more.

"She has to see you at your most magnificent!" Ken said, wagging a lone finger in the air. "Something to show her what she's missing out on by not being with you."

Hence the painting. The painting, which would show me as I might one day be. Something to give form to all I had inside me, if only the opportunity would present itself. We were so serious about it. So exuberant. So sure it would happen. We were young enough to still believe ideas born late at night could survive the dawn. If you had asked me that night, I would have said the painting was a 100 percent certainty. All we had to do was find an oil painter, scrounge up some cash, and tell him what to do. When she received the painting in the mail, she'd immediately welcome me back.

The next day, we woke up, drove to our friend's wolf sanctuary and home, and picked up Bengal, a little, orange pit bull with black tiger stripes traversing her smelly, muscular body. With her and a 30-pack of more inexpensive beer, we headed to a remote river in the middle of the woods, where the cold, clear, rushing waters swelled, slowed, and formed a lagoon.

There, we sat on the shore and threw large sticks, over and over, into the water. Again and again, the little dog bounded into the stream, snatched the wood in her jaws, and returned. We had little to escape. No kids, no debt that would come due anytime soon. The kinds of jobs that, if we never showed up again, would simply find another imbecile. But the very act of escaping, even if there was no real monster pursuing us, still felt good as we sat by the water, belched, and talked about a book I had just read called *A Man in Full*, in which you quickly realize that wealthy, powerful people are just as scared of the dark as the rest of us.

With the afternoon light came a slender young stranger, her legs tan and her underarms sprouting the kind of prickly stubble I hoped would one day accentuate the cowardly curvature of my jaw. She came out of nowhere, quietly and happily, sitting down next to us and joining the conversation. She threw the stick, never cringing when the soggy, slithering dog body slapped against her, and drank beer. She told us she was leaving the following morning, going to Utah. She had no plans, nothing waiting for her, and little to leave behind except the banality of her life.

For those hours, every conversation—and in those conversations every sentence, every word, every nod of the head and every silence—fit together perfectly. There was no biding your time while the other person spoke, just waiting to say something that might make you seem clever. No. Everything fit. Nearly every declaration, every time, was met with a two-person chorus: "Yes!"

"So you're just leaving?" Ken asked.

"Mmm, hm," she said with a smile and a nod, her tank top splattered by mud and little brown droplets of water from the dog's frenetic wriggling.

"I wish I could do that," I lamented. "Just leave."

"Me too," said Ken.

"Why can't you?" she asked. "You should come with me. You can ride in my car. Just come."

When I was a little boy, I used to imagine that I could fly, but I just didn't know it yet. The only reason I had never taken off, I dreamed, was that I had never really been aware that I could do it. Someday I would realize I could, and away I would flap.

Maybe this was a similar situation.

"Okay," I said.

"Okay," Ken agreed.

As the sun descended, we went over the logistics. She would pick us up the next morning, at the end of the dead-end road where we had parked to walk down to the river.

As we left that day, tired and content and free, we embraced tightly, the rims of our eyes red with tears, and vowed to return in a few hours. On the way back to Ken's house, we chatted on and on about how free we would feel as we barreled toward Utah.

The next morning, we slept in.

Our journey into the unknown was the prior day's painting, relegated forever to the magical land of hypothetical possibility, where people can fly, and they just don't know it yet.

UGLY KID MATT

My mom played so much Enya when I was a kid. Her songs were grandiose, pulsating, sentimental, and aggressively feminine. I couldn't understand what she was saying—she was singing in Gaelic or Elvish or something—so I really didn't know. But the violins and synthesizers, which were relentless, were perfectly clear, and they were chanting: "Uterus!"

For my dad, music wasn't something you paired with other activities. These days, people listen to music all the time, streaming it through their phones while they drive, half-heartedly listening while they do dishes, or even on the phone while they go to the bathroom. But for my dad, it was an intimate affair. He only listened to music in private. No one else could be around to disturb him.

As Neil Young's haunting vocals soared over soft guitar strums, my father, in his favorite chair, sat with his eyes closed, escaping into the music. He listened so intently he seemed to completely leave his body. For him, music was not a side dish; it was the main course. When you were listening to it, that was all you should be doing. When he entered my bedroom and found me on my back, on the top bunk, a few inches from the ceiling, lying on blue and gold Batman sheets while I listened to '90s rap, chewed grape bubblegum, and read a *Hardy Boys* book, he felt like he was seeing a cat driving a car while it did long division and clipped its nails.

Sometimes, during a listening session, he'd sense I was nearby and open one eye. "Come in here and listen to this music with me!" he'd yell over a chugging guitar riff. "Sit down over there and listen! Isn't this great!"

Sitting in a chair and feeling the incredibly loud music in my lower intestine, I always wondered: "Now what? Is this it?"

I felt like it was dinner time and my dad was happy to feast exclusively on ketchup. "Shouldn't," I asked him when the song was over, "this go along with something else?"

The songs my parents listened to were very different. But all their music did the same thing—it allowed them to escape the narrow confines of time and space. My mother's New Age Celtic pop added romance to a life populated primarily by farm animals and a little boy who couldn't be left alone without starting a grease fire or clogging a toilet. My father's rock was a loophole that allowed him to completely leave the premises without technically being guilty of parental negligence.

At the age of 12, in 1992, I purchased a cassette featuring a song called *Cat's in the Cradle*. The artist, Ugly Kid Joe, was a pop heavy-metal group whose prior hit featured the juvenile, but undeniably catchy, chorus, "I hate everything about you." Their new song, on the other hand, was as syrupy and sentimental as humanly possible.

Originally a folk song in the 1970s, Ugly Kid Joe gave *Cat's in the Cradle* the full pop metal treatment. If Enya's music channeled the essence of sensual femininity, Ugly Kid Joe did the same thing with the spirit of boogers and farts.

Yet somehow, their rendition of the song genuinely moved me.

It is about a dad who, due to work, misplaced priorities, a little bit of apathy and a general inability to grasp the concept that life is fleeting and everyone grows up, never finds time for his son. He's away on business when the child takes his first steps, and he can't find the time to play a simple game of catch. In the end, the roles are reversed. The father, who you assume is doddering and lonely, calls his son on the phone, only to discover that the younger man doesn't have time for him. "Ah, bitter irony," you think.

For some reason it hammered a chord in my heart. I think most boys my age heard it. Today, as we approach 40 and raise children of our own, it's clearly manifesting itself in our parenting styles.

It's a testament to the power of music that half a million adolescent boys purchased a single that was essentially a lecture about parenting. If you sat me down and told me "do unto others as you would have them do unto you," or "don't completely ignore your kid," I probably would have zoned out. But when a bunch of boozy L.A. morons with shaggy hair and less-than-inspired albums like *Ugly As They Wanna Be* and *America's Least Wanted* sang about it, I really heard them. I remember pledging, with blazing eyes and a swollen throat, that I would never make the same mistake as the father in that song.

Sometimes my wife calls me while I'm at work. It's usually to make sure our schedules are properly aligned, or to ask why there are coffee grounds all over the kitchen. Our toddler often grabs the phone and starts talking to me.

Once, at 1:30 p.m. on a Tuesday, I heard what sounded like a brief scuffle followed by her breathy voice on the phone. She sounded like her face was pressed up pretty firmly against the receiver. "Come home and make pancakes with me? Do puzzles?"

Then I heard the phone fall to the floor, and the sound of a little person running away, presumably to taunt the cat. I respond to this type of thing in exactly the same way I would if she told me our house were on fire. I literally run out the door of my office—leaving behind an unsaved story on my computer and a stack of things that were supposed to get done that day—and I dash to my car.

"I have to go," I cry behind me as I run, coatless into a blizzard outside. "It's an emergency!"

In those moments, if someone told me I might be fired for going home to make pancakes or do puzzles, I wouldn't comprehend what they were talking about.

"If you want me to be the *Cat's in the Cradle* dad, you've got another thing coming," I'd say. I think that's okay.

Because soon, my daughter won't care if I come home to bake with her. Soon, she'll be a teenager and actively not want me to come home, so she can spend all her time doing things I wouldn't allow if I were in the building.

But when that day arrives, I can always find a comfortable chair somewhere and take a seat. Then I'll blast music and my mind can go wherever it wants, free from the constraints of time and space. I know it will race back to the good old days, the best ones of my life, which I spent flipping pancakes and putting together puzzles.

EXISTENTIAL CHRISTMAS

I judge each child I meet based on her or his merits. I don't always end up liking them, but at least those who receive my love have done something to deserve it. I'm not the only one who does.

On my daughter's third Christmas, we strolled with her down to the public library to see Santa, a man famous for judging kids. Child after child plopped down on his lap to ask for an assortment of plastic things. Little did they know Santa wasn't the only one judging them on that particular morning.

"Ho, ho, ho," he said, really chewing on the limited dialogue. "What do you want for Christmas this year?"

"I have a Christmas tree, and a cat, and some snow, and some cookies," Hadley replied proudly. "I have a mom and a dad at my house." It's possible she just misheard or misunderstood the question. She is three, after all. But I took it as a sign of her moral superiority. She didn't want more stuff. She was already happy—proud, in fact—with what she had.

I glanced behind me to make sure the other parents were listening. Parenting is a competition, of course, and I was winning. I could've headed home and let her light off some fireworks while she smoked a cigar, and I still would've been the best dad around, at least on that particular day.

I stood up to leave when she was done, and my knees creaked audibly under the strain. I was getting fat again, after all.

* * * * *

A couple of years earlier, I decided to lose some weight. I stopped eating things everyone knows make you fat, and subsequently lost 60 pounds. Everyone thought I was dying. For some people—and apparently I fall squarely into this category—being thin brings with it distinct aesthetic unpleasantness. Like an emaciated, sallow-faced Santa Claus, my newfound leanness robbed me of my more jolly attributes.

"Are you okay?" people asked.

"I just stopped eating sugary things and drinking beer," I said, stroking my beard. "I also stopped eating cheese, which is nice because dairy wreaks havoc on my stomach."

I live in Wisconsin. I might as well have said I lost the weight running ultra-marathons with my pet unicorn. In space.

"That can't be right," they all said. "Are you sure you're okay?"

So I panicked. I decided to gain back a few pounds. By December, I once again found myself round and jolly, just like that most famous judger of children.

People think Santa is meant to teach kids that if you're good, you'll be rewarded. He's not. The story of Santa is a myth, and like any mythology, its power does not rely on any of its components being literally true. In fact, mythologies are more powerful, more universal and more alive, because they have been created, almost magically, out of nothing.

And he is real. After all, someone had to put all those presents in the stockings. Someone had to gobble all those cookies, even though his doctor recently told him to lose some weight, and guzzle all that milk, even though he's lactose intolerant. A big-bellied man with a long beard and a bellowing laugh, who lives in a very cold place full of snow and ice.

I can't honestly tell my daughter he loves all children, but I can look her in the eye and swear that he loves her. I'll tell her he loves her because he knows her, and therefore he knows she is worthy of love.

THIS IS FUNNY

Along a shrub-lined isthmus of secluded sidewalk near our elementary school, they lurked and prowled. They were paunchy, with wrinkled clothing and dark, prickly facial hair jaundiced by a perpetual haze of cigarette smoke. They were the imaginary serial murderers from whom I dreamed of rescuing my classmates and teachers.

Unfortunately, crime wasn't much of a concern in the small New England community I was raised in. But tragedy and death arrive in many forms; they merely put on different outfits when they leave the house to meet with the privileged. My town was a place of suicides and falls from expensive horses, the sorts of tragedies superheroes don't usually help with.

The villains I dreamed up and then imagined protecting my classmates from were only there to elicit fear. It wouldn't be traumatic enough to do any permanent psychological damage. This would be roughly equivalent to someone entering a room behind you while you were vacuuming, causing a sensation of terror and relief that came in such quick succession they might as well have been two parts of the same emotion.

I was always there to save the would-be victim.

"Not today!" I'd declare, emerging from a bush or from behind a nearby Volvo. Now that I'm better with language, I realize such a catch-phrase, even when uttered from the lips of a vigilante, could imply that the abduction or assault had merely been delayed, rather than permanently stopped. This, of course, was the result of a loose grasp on language, not any intent on my part for harm to befall anyone in the future. What I should have yelled, of course, was "Never!"

My emergence was usually enough to fix everything. My braided rat tail flowing in the breeze behind me like a billowing cape, I would stand with my legs apart, as if I had just hopped off a horse, and the thug would flee. The girl, boy, or teacher, who until then had treated me with scorn, would run to me, shedding the elementary school caste system and throwing loving arms around a boy who until then had been no one.

Sometimes that wasn't enough. Sometimes the imaginary criminals didn't run, and I was forced to bludgeon them with my pale, soft, little fists until they howled and screamed for mercy, which was always good for a laugh that lightened the mood and made the person I was saving think, "Wow, Matt is funny, too!"

These opportunities never materialized on their own. Would our low crime rate force me to stage an attack? Perhaps I would have to play both villain and hero in this charade. I could dress up as a rogue and jump out of the bushes myself, then quickly disappear. After a quick costume change, with the fake dirt scrubbed from my cheeks and the pea-green army jacket discarded out of sight, I would re-emerge as myself and save the day.

"Is everything okay over here," I'd say. "I didn't like the looks of that guy."

It was always around this point in the daydream that I realized I had gone, far too quickly, from fantasizing about being a superhero to fantasizing about being the type of person from whom superheroes protect innocent people. The fantasies tended to be abandoned mid-stream as I was flooded by shame. In that direction lurked psychological dragons with whom I did not wish to do battle.

Yet I yearned for one of those moments. A single instant in which a person or people suddenly saw me in a completely new, far more flattering way. I always had bags under my eyes, and I was usually uninterested in whatever was being taught at school, so the widespread impression of me was that I looked like a dim-witted slug.

There were worse first impressions to give, like the boy who had fallen on a stick in such a way that a surprisingly large section of it became lodged and eventually completely sealed within the skin on his face. It moved about, from day to day, week to week, and month to month, searching for a way out—like a seal trying with increasing desperation to find an air hole in the ice. The stick would poke and prod, just enough to cause a nasty red bulb to appear on the boy's cheek, but it could never muster the strength to break through every layer of skin and gain its freedom.

I had no sticks in my face, but my lack of coordination and speed on the playground, coupled with my oafish answers in the classroom, rendered me wholly unimpressive. I needed something dramatic to happen—something that could, as in alchemy, take a dull and gray thing and make it shimmer.

* * * * *

A couple of years later, after being sent to a private school where people were far more afraid of insider trading charges than of scruffy attackers, I was required to write a story. I was perpetually teased in school, by classmates and teachers alike, for my prose. I wrote a series of tales about a pair of mice who lived on a farm and liked to play baseball together, until one of them was eventually eaten by a cat. It seemed real enough—cats and mice and farms and baseball all existed in my life. But it wasn't pretentious enough for little kids raised on bedtime tales by Nathaniel Hawthorne, for readers to whom Michael Dukakis was the closest thing to a jock they had ever seen on television.

At the end of the semester, we had to compose one last story to read aloud at a salon attended by parents, administrators, and teachers. I sat down to write another rodent-based tragedy, but I found it difficult to concentrate. My mind was fixated on a prank my parents had played on me at Christmas, filling my stocking with coal and pretending not to give me the toy Batmobile—complete with bright yellow foam rockets—that I had been begging for, for months.

My dad couldn't stop laughing. Inebriated by the charade's power, his entire head seemed to be smiling as I cried and screamed and threatened to run away.

"Maybe," he said as if offering a piece of sage wisdom, "it's these kinds of temper tantrums that made Santa put the coal in your stocking in the first place."

"Stop laughing!" I demanded.

"What do you want me to do?" he said. "This is funny."

What could he do, really? It was funny, and you can't not laugh at something funny any more than you can *not* cry when the doctor shows you the pale, ghostly MRI slice of a tumor.

When I finally calmed down, my dad pretended to find a large, rectangular package behind the couch. "Ah, jeez; looks like Santa did leave you a present after all."

So instead of a Batmobile that Christmas, I got a Batmobile and a story. I played with the Batmobile for a week, then lost the yellow rockets and left the vehicle itself outside in the snow, where the plastic grew brittle and eventually shattered when I tripped on it that spring.

The story lasted longer. I wrote it down, exactly as I thought it happened. Then I read it to all the parents, administrators, and teachers who gathered at the end of the semester. They were all so bored, I noticed as I waited for my turn to stand up and read, and no amount of tweed in the room or money in their bank accounts could fix that. One girl who had only recently learned to tie shoelaces read an exhaustive piece about the economic impact of Castro's agricultural reforms in Cuba. We were in hell.

They needed a hero. Someone to step out of the shadows and rescue them. My story was riddled with typos, inconsistencies, and a narrative arc that was uneven at best. It was about a little boy who looked a bit like a slug, performed poorly at school and in sports, and girls tended not to notice. But somewhere, deep down, there was something good in him. And so, when he got coal in his stocking, the adults laughed and laughed. Not at him, but in agreement with him. Their chuckles and guffaws were, at the very least, an acknowledgement that his grievances were legitimate. The way, when you laugh at someone who takes a soccer ball to the groin, you are really saying, "Yes, that does hurt."

Together, we ascended from hell.

And in that instant, I knew they saw me in a new light. Standing there, sweating, fidgeting with my papers, and trying to keep my voice from cracking, I shimmered and dazzled.

My parents were smiling, too, but their faces also expressed terror.

"Why are you doing this?" their eyes pleaded.

As I continued my story, I shot them a quick glance. "What do you want me to do?" it said. "This is funny."

LITTLE DIPPER BOY

One muggy summer afternoon in 1983, I squeezed into a pair of slick blue tights, a shirt with an oversized large red and yellow patch stitched to the front, and a flowing red cape. I clambered into my parents' green Peugeot and was off with my dad to the movie theater in a nearby town.

My dad believed that death, taxes, and torturous movie theater seats are the only "inevitables" in life. To be driven to the movies by such a man was incredibly rare.

"But, Dad," I said recently. "Movie theaters these days are filled with plush recliners. They're controlled by a digital system that lets you put up a huge, soft footrest and lie almost flat. Like a bed, but with cup holders and a spot where you can stow candy and beer!"

"Ehh," he replied, shifting in a creaky, threadbare, analog La-Z-Boy in his living room. "Still sounds uncomfortable to me."

He had a point—back in 1983. But for me, it was a glorious place. The red velvet. The self-playing piano in the lobby. The strange, unlabeled little plastic containers of drinks that came in colors, rather than flavors.

Inside the theater, with the lights pleasantly softening the edges of the world my eyes took in, I tucked my cape beneath my legs and prepared to watch Superman vanquish evil. A few minutes later, both Superman and Matt

Geiger learned, for the first time, of something called Red Kryptonite. It makes Superman smash cars and terrify innocent people. It makes him evil. Its effect on Matt Geiger is even more severe. It causes him to stand up, head for the aisle, and exit the theater in a single bound.

"Matt, where are you going?!" my dad cried out in the unnatural amalgamation of a whisper and a yell. "The movie just started . . ."

I was already on my way into the lobby.

"Don't you want to go back and watch the rest of the movie?" he asked when he caught up with me, and in his eyes, I saw him slowly, surely assembling the pieces of a weird, little psychological puzzle.

"I, I . . ." I stuttered.

Before I could think of anything better to say, my dad cut me off. "You know what? That chair was really starting to hurt my back."

Just for show, I pretended to waver. "Yeah, but we already paid for the tickets, and I still have a few sips of purple left and—"

"No," he cut in again. "I'm sorry, but I really should get home and milk the cows. Do you want to help me milk the cows? You can put the iodine on their teats. It would really help me out."

And with a few simple words about a cow's nipples, a vast cosmos of fear and anxiety vanished. It's always such a surprise when this cosmos lifts, because no matter how many times it happens, fear always feels eternal, while the joy that serves as its counterbalance always, even at its highest points, feels so painfully fleeting. But, oh, how well I could breathe again.

So the women behind the counter, snapping their gum and chatting amongst themselves, glimpsed—through a fog of smoke from the barely controlled burning of canola oil, and over a display case full of chocolates and fruit-flavored candies—a little boy, flying away to help his father fight the terrible crime of bovine mastitis.

THE BAREFOOT PUGILIST

I just watched a 75-year-old woman engage in the most elegant pugilistic ritual, wrapping her knuckles in black gauze before stuffing them into her gloves. She has Parkinson's disease, so her hands, both the one being wrapped and the one doing the wrapping, trembled while she did it. The next thing I know, she's up in the ring, jumping rope. That's followed by a round of shadow boxing, then one-on-one time with her trainer, then a sweaty session on the heavy bag.

The gym is full of boxers, all of whom share two things in common: their neurodegenerative disease and their love of boxing. Call it elegance, call it muscle memory, the woman is quick-witted and sharp-tongued, teasing me before she climbs into the ring.

Parkinson's brought them to a boxing gym populated mostly by aspiring young fighters and thick-necked body-builders. Like all such places, the music competes with the erratic, ceaseless clanging of weights.

My little old lady calls it "a place of great emotional energy."

"We're all deteriorating," she says. "But this helps."

I think she's referring to the Parkinson's, but she could be talking about all of us. We're all dying, after all. All deteriorating as we trundle toward the grave.

There's a former nun and a retired high school teacher. There's a grandfather who brings his 13-year-old grandson, who is also learning to box. The elder got a heavy bag for Christmas, and he hung it in his basement, where he and his child's child descend to throw combinations. As he works the speed bag today, he whiffs—it's something that could happen to anyone, with or without Parkinson's—and he grins and looks over at me: "What did I miss?"

One boxer, clear words tumbling through trembling lips, talks about how much better he feels after these sessions. They don't hit, or get hit, in the head. But they do everything else. "Sometimes people fall down," he says with a smile. Then they get back up.

On another night, I meet other boxers. Ones driven into the gym by other ghosts and demons and emotional quagmires.

One of them tells me a secret: "There's no irony in boxing."

I'm sitting on the outer edge of the ring, my right arm draped over the bottom rope, when "The Professor" tells me this. A scholar of French who used to teach at a nearby university, he's middle-aged, thin, and erudite.

"Every obstacle, my whole life, I was like water, I just went around it," he explains. He's so drenched in sweat from sparring that the dark gray moisture threatens to wipe out a small, resilient archipelago of remaining dry spots on his shirt. "I wanted to learn to stand my ground. I wanted to learn to go through something, just once."

According to "Jersey No-Foot" Eddie, the Professor now throws a great jab.

Eddie has big, empathetic eyes and the kind of honest enthusiasm most people lose by the time they reach the age of 12. The first time I saw him fight, at a tournament in a crowded bar, his foot fell off. It happened after he took a hard punch from his opponent, stepping back only to have his leg come loose just above the shin.

Watching the match from the side of the ring, I had no idea his right foot and ankle, which were shoved into a typical boxing boot secured by a latticework of laces, were prosthetic.

"Oh, my God!" I thought. "That guy got punched so hard his foot fell off." I swallowed hard and added this information to my already large and eclectic list of concerns. Car crashes. Skin cancer. Deforestation caused by my consumption of foods containing palm oil. And now this—the real possibility that if someone ever punched me in the face, one of my appendages might come flying off.

Eddie hopped back to his corner and put his foot back on. Then he headed back to the center of the ring. Then he kept fighting. Even after I figured out what had happened, I couldn't wrap my mind around this kind of intestinal fortitude. I'd quit fighting if my hat fell off. I once went home from work for the day because, as I moaned to a friend, "my lips were way too chapped."

* * * * *

My first—and final—foray into the ring took place when I was still a child. My mother, having recently enrolled me in tap-dancing classes, realized I'd need to defend myself on the playground, so she also signed me up for taekwondo.

My teacher—my *sa bum*—stressed that we were not really learning to fight. We were learning how to move and how to control our minds and bodies. Ultimately, he said we were learning how to live a better life. I made it to the modest rank of yellow belt, with a strip of torn brown tape wrapped around it. The tape suggested modest progress toward the next color in the rainbow of martial arts waist-wear. I suspect it also signified that my mom's checks had continued to arrive on time for several weeks.

Taekwondo culture exists in a place where the color of a person's belt directly represents how dangerous they are. Not far removed from a world where your hat indicates how adept you are at math, and your shoes tell people how fast you can run. I was told that once you grew better at fighting, your master would give you a new belt. But I always wondered if the system could be cheated; if, perhaps, wearing a brown or black belt would magically make me tougher.

My parents selected taekwondo because it was of Korean origin. Just like my little sister. As if it would give us something in common. This was why we frequently traveled to Korean restaurants in Boston—in case my sister, who came to our family as a squalling infant—might take a bite of spicy fermented cabbage and say, "This really brings me back."

The taekwondo lessons took place on a warped parquet floor in front of a wall-length mirror. The stench of every-one's feet was overwhelming. I wanted to learn to fight in a verdant bamboo grove, or perhaps on a snowy mountain top, thanks to the aesthetic ideas I'd picked up from cartoons. Not a place pervaded by the crotch-and-toe smell of a middle-school locker room.

Our instructor's name was Bruce—yet another in an increasingly long string of disappointments about the realities of martial arts. "Master Bruce" would never sound right to my ear. Years later, a friend pointed out that "Master Bruce" is what Alfred the butler calls Batman. But this guy drove a Pontiac, not a Batmobile, so I suspect there was no relation.

He was kind and patient. Most importantly, he wore a different color belt than I did, so I knew he could beat me up. The belt said so, and I was in no position to argue.

He spoke of the importance of forms, breathing, and philosophy. In my bedroom at home, I practiced the methodical, plodding, slow-motion combat he showed us. I was often timid and introspective at school, I tended to worry more than other kids did, and my chest was sunken and weak. I was always asking questions, which everyone, school teachers most of all, found annoying.

Maybe taekwondo would fix everything. Perhaps if I mastered my breathing, working for hours on end at the forms, like Master Bruce said, I'd find my inner strength and be filled with radiant courage. Maybe the ability to kill, or at the very least maim, was the thing I needed to turn my life around.

Then it ended. We rode to our first tournament, where I was placed into a ring and made to fight another boy. He reeked of corn-syrupy soft drinks and fast-food hamburgers, which I now understand contain a lot of residual steroids. For him, taekwondo wasn't about philosophy or forms. It was about kicking and punching, hard and fast. He hit so hard! And at regular speed, not the slow motion we always used when practicing our forms. I was sure he was about to smash a bottle and insert its jagged, malty green teeth into my gut with a twist. We'd never met before, but he came at me like a well-compensated assassin.

As blood gushed from my nose, I realized I had nothing against this boy. I didn't disagree with him over politics or religion. We weren't even in love with the same girl. We were just from different towns, we were both wearing white pajamas with yellow belts, and we had both been placed in a ring, like a pair of pre-pubescent roosters, and told to fight.

"I mean you no harm!" I shouted as he punched and kicked me to the ground. My overly theatrical cry gave him renewed strength. Up until then, he'd been unsure of the social rank of the boy he was pummeling. But my words, confirming my status as a nerd, proved to him that striking me was correct. My defense was about as effective as shouting, "Don't eat me, I'm just a delicious baby antelope!" to a ravenous lioness.

I didn't land a single blow. When it was over, I was happy to be alive, but also unhappy to have been attacked and beaten in a gymnasium on a Saturday morning. The other kid received a hug and a trophy. I was given some shame and a bag of ice that smelled strongly of freezer burn.

"Mom, Dad," I said from the back of the car on the way home. "I don't want to do taekwondo anymore."

"We know, boy," my dad said with a sigh. "We could tell."

"I don't really want to do tap dance anymore, either," I added. I wanted to quit everything.

"Well, I don't think they should have let you fight against such a strong boy," my mom said, finding just the right words to make me feel a little worse.

After that, I became a pacifist. It was a good fit, rationalizing my cowardice and providing an outlet for my slothful nature. I was pleased with myself for being able to couch my inaction neatly into a morally lofty philosophical trope.

I chose not to fight because I didn't like getting punched. Not punching other people reduced the chances of retaliation. I said I chose not to fight because I was better than those who did—the general idea was that my muscles and testicles might be smaller than everyone else's, but my moral compass was much, much bigger. Maybe, as if applying a little mascara and a fancy wig made from the hairs of dead, moral philosophers, I could dress up my cowardice as virtue.

* * * * *

Andrea is a retired pro boxer. Today, she trains others how to fight, including the men and women with Parkinson's, The Professor and Eddie, and even a couple boxers aiming for the Olympics. She walks with a grace I've only seen in fighters, as if those around her are laboring sluggishly through a bog. When she walks toward me, a big smile showing a row of fake teeth, her ponytail bobbing as it rushes to keep up, it seems like even the air parts before her, choosing, just like me, that sometimes it's better not to put up a fight. Hers is not the kind of abstract grace mused about by poets and painters. It's more immediate, inexorably linked to mind, muscle, and matter. It's the kind of grace you can put on a scale and weigh, or wrap a tape around and measure.

"In the ring, you have to be smart," says one of her most promising fighters after a round of sparring. Then he stops to correct his verbiage, waving his prior words out of the air with a big blue glove that only seconds before was battering someone's face: "You can't be dumb."

In a world where stupidity is not only allowed, but enthusiastically encouraged, this little 16-foot-by-20-foot square, where idiocy has consequences that include the temporary loss of consciousness, sounds downright utopian.

Here, if you do something moronic, you get your nose broken. Things should be like this in the House of Representatives.

Everyone who trains under Andrea, whether driven to the sport by Parkinson's, pugilistic ambition, or existential crisis, speaks of her the same way. To them, she's part teacher, part benevolent tyrant, part sage. When she's circling them in the gym, telling them how and when to strike, the sweat almost smells like a verdant bamboo grove.

In addition to being a former pro boxer, she's also a black belt in multiple forms of martial arts. Her social media handle is "BarefootPugilist," because she restores prairies and likes to garden with her feet in the soil.

"I thought it was clever," she says with a shrug and smile. "I don't think anyone knows what it means though."

The daughter of a college professor, she had her own reasons for entering the ring. She got into trouble as a teen, and hooked up with an abusive boyfriend. It's a difficult idea to come to terms with. To think of someone who used to get paid to beat up professional fighters, someone on whose expertise up-and-coming boxers now depend, as the victim of anything. But love, or the illusion of it, allows all variants of evil to lurk and thrive in its shadows.

One night, after Andrea tried to leave her boyfriend, she says he broke into her home and tried to kill her. He later went to prison for an unrelated crime. She eventually escaped that relationship. But even after she became a boxer, she experienced Post Traumatic Stress Disorder.

"One day, when he was getting out of prison, they called me to inform me—I was on a list or whatever—and I started to feel it," she explains. "This is after I was a boxer. But I could feel it. Then I realized: he's just a person."

"So, did you ever imagine his face on your opponents in the ring?" I ask. "Just see his face on them and smash it?"

"No, nothing like that," she says, looking into the ring. "They're just targets trying to hit you. The demons you face in there, they're not exactly people."

The past and the future shatter and disperse. You are left with only the present. The night your ex-boyfriend tried to murder you? You must leave that memory, and the place you once were no longer dictates the person you are now. You must leave the future, too. You have more important things to deal with.

A boxer once told me we are all deteriorating. It's true; we are all bundles of dying cells, some of which make up a brain that's blessed and cursed with the ability to fathom our universal and inevitable descent into non-existence. But when your hands are taped and stuffed into gloves, and you step through the ropes, you are alive, and your demon, your opponent, is standing naked in front of you, no longer lurking, no longer formless and terrifying in the shadows.

Right there, bathed under the bright lights, your enemy is illuminated. You remember your training, you keep your hands up, you keep your stance wide (never long). You get a good look at your demon, exposed by the lights, and you think, "That's not so bad."

COFFEE

Early this morning, I grabbed my reporter's notebook, several pens in the hopes that one of them might contain some liquid ink, and what can quite accurately be described as a pond of black coffee.

I sat down on the deck, immersed in that beautiful, upended rainstorm that takes place each summer morning, when the dew on the grass starts to sizzle and fall miraculously back up into the heavens. I was ready to conduct a phone interview, but after several moments, I had to admit something was wrong.

"Why isn't this working?" I asked myself, puzzled as usual. "I have my notebook, I have my pen, I'm spilling boiling coffee all over my shorts just like always. What's missing?"

My phone. Right.

I had left it somewhere inside, rendering a phone interview nearly impossible. I had to go back in anyway, to get more coffee, since I had spilled all of mine.

"I might as well get a new notebook while I'm in there," I thought to myself, watching the first pad of paper slowly sop up a pool of dark, Peruvian, caffeinated liquid.

I recently mentioned to a friend that perhaps, just maybe, I drink too much coffee.

"How much do you typically drink?" he asked.

"Maybe a little less than 12 ounces each day," I replied.

"That's not much. That's not even two cups."

"No, I mean a 12-ounce bag of dry coffee," I explained. "The bag says it makes 62 cups."

"Oh!"

I'm not sure if my coffee consumption means I'm going to live forever, or die tomorrow. I'm fairly certain it will be through one of those two doors I pass, as I tend to divide my health concerns and fantasies into those very extreme categories. I do like to point out that I'm often drinking coffee in lieu of other things, primarily Scotch, gin, and rocket fuel, which is a factor that should be considered when its net impact on my life is calculated.

The thing about coffee is that there is an abundance of science about its effects, but many of the studies seem to disprove other studies. I was even told that until recently, the World Health Organization classified it as having both carcinogenic and anti-carcinogenic properties, which means coffee sellers could boast that their product both causes and prevents cancer.

I recently read about an expansive study that showed people in Spain who drink lots of coffee (and I do mean lots) live for much longer than those who don't. I'm 39 now, so I decided that's where my investigation into the impact of coffee on my health will end. I'm going to move on to other areas of inquiry, about the gray hairs that are sprouting in my beard and the fact that I've recently discovered that all movies and music are either far too loud or inaudibly quiet, with no middle ground.

We all know how this ends, with me, 40 years from now, sipping a cup of coffee while I read an Internet article about new findings regarding incontinence, nodding in grim agreement.

* * * * *

When you are very young, you are always searching for new findings. You tend to get excited when you discover that what everyone who came before you thought turned out to be wrong.

"Actually, they now know that the Black Plague was actually caused by clarinets," you explain to puzzled older people. "And that the *Tyrannosaurus rex* was kind of a mauve color, with polka dots, and it ate only butterflies and sunflowers seeds."

In my darker moments, I start to wonder why we bother learning anything at all in our younger years. Ninety percent of what I was taught as a child has since been proven incorrect or obsolete. That metric system the U.S. was planning to transition to in the year 1989. The number of planets. Whether or not eggs are good for you or bad for you (and on a related note, the very nature of cholesterol). It recently came to my attention that some prick decided to completely change math.

In the 1990s, everyone, and I do mean everyone, was convinced that fat was causing everyone's health problems. Every type of food on the shelf started to come in "low-fat" varieties. Then everyone found out that fat alone might not have been the culprit, and that some fats might in fact prevent the diseases they were worried about, so everyone in the country spent a decade cramming avocados into their mouths and following it up with a tankard of olive oil.

When I was a kid, everything had sugar in it. Then, suddenly, nothing had sugar in it, as it was replaced by artificial sweeteners. Then, when people discovered those fake sugars might be harmful, cereals and soft drinks switched BACK to sugar, even boasting about it on their labels. "Contains real cane sugar!"

My dad, who is nearing 70 and therefore has been dealing with this back-and-forth swing of knowledge for 30 more years than I have, recently summed it up better than I ever could.

"You should take lots of vitamin C if you feel like you are getting a cold," he told me last winter. "Unless that's been disproven now. Has that been disproven yet? Even if it has, I'm sure it will get proven again, eventually."

Like Nietzsche, he is becoming convinced that this is not a linear process. It is a circular one.

I think that's why I remain so committed to the things that we know we will never truly understand. That's why I love the things that exist only in the ether, but profoundly impact our lives. Things like love, beauty, ethics, and art. Because unlike eggs, coffee, sugar, and fat, we can't ever really quantify them or their effects on us. They are invisible, yet real, and we know that while we do not fully understand them, they will always be with us.

THE MONKEYS OF NEW ENGLAND

When you get monkeys, the story is always the same. They're cute and cuddly, and they act like adorable little fur people. Then they hit monkey puberty.

Suddenly, things change.

Legend had it that the old English woman who lived in the spooky Gothic mansion had gotten her monkeys when they were little. She lived just down the gravel path that ambled between two stone horse paddocks. In that genteel house, which existed in the realm somewhere between living quarters and museum exhibit, monkeys climbed on towering bookshelves, clasping the ostentatious golden edges of oil paintings as they swung along the wall.

They dozed on worn leather furniture lush with the odor of saddle soap. They harassed a menagerie of cats and dogs. They were furry, living reminders that no matter how much Earl Grey we drink or how much gilt we put on the edges of our editions of Shakespeare, we all only recently descended from the trees.

Sooner or later, like most primates, they staged a rebellion. Unable to make demands, there was no way to placate them. They had no Caesar, no union rep, no ambassador with an embassy in the human world. At some point, they were moved into the basement. There they lived, hooting and hollering, with food tossed down to them, for a while, until a plumber came to fix a pipe. When they bit him, it was clear they had to go.

When I was a child, I always wondered what those first few monkey-less days and nights must have been like. The silence must have been deafening. All the old woman could do was sit there with her pet crow perched atop her shoulder, as the primates' pungent aroma slowly, tragically began to fade.

The crow, I was told, would often glide into town, where it met her when she drove to the post office to pick up her mail. Perhaps it was two crows, now that I think of it.

And perhaps it wasn't the mail, because there was a man who did that. His name was Mario. He had thick, permanently tanned, wrinkled skin and white hair always covered by a mesh-backed baseball cap. His job, as far as I could tell, was to retrieve the mail from the post office, and to bring it to us, and to the Englishwoman, and to take as long as possible doing it.

He was a talker, and one of my earliest memories involves my mother clamping her hand over my mouth and pulling me violently to her side, as my father quickly drew the blinds and slumped down beneath the window sill. They moved with the urgency of people trying to avoid the gaze of a sniper.

"Sshhh," my dad whispered as he held a warning finger to his lips. Outside, Mario rapped on the door. A moment later, he dislodged his hat so he could press his face up to the window glass.

"We're nice people," my dad protested after Mario sauntered off. "It's just that we really don't have time to talk to him right now. There's not enough time to talk to him and do everything else that needs to be done on the farm today."

* * * * *

My memories of these things are vague and dreamlike. The characters are not specific people, but archetypes. They are like Batman and the Joker, who lived inside hundreds of comic books illustrated by dozens of different artists, each with their own style. Sometimes Batman was brawny and squat, with short horns on his cowl, and sometimes he was lithe and wispy, with a billowing cape 30 feet long. But he was always Batman.

The old Englishwoman, and the talkative mailman, who clearly had no legal affiliation with the United States Postal Service, and my mom and dad and sister, and even me—we all are like that. We are loose, formless ideas. We each possess something essential, but it's all buried deep within, beneath layer after layer of malleable forms.

At different times in my life, I have been small, and huge. I have been young, and I have been middle-aged. I have been extroverted, and I have been terrified to leave the house. I have been the dumbest person in the room, so dull that I made those around me dumber. At other times, I was the most clever person in the crowd—like Falstaff, I was not only clever myself, but so radiant in my insights that I was also the cause of wit in other people. Yet somehow, it is all me.

What is it that makes me, me? What exactly is a "Matt Geiger"? I know what he does, at least I do after he does things. But the thing I see, when I see myself, seems to be merely the flickering, dancing shadow of something far more real, which exists just outside of my line of vision. Is a monkey that cute little thing that sits on your shoulder and swings from the chandeliers? Or is it the slightly larger thing that screeches through the night and urinates on your poodle? The answer is—both.

The average speaker of English has a vocabulary of about 40,000 words, but at least half of them are passive. That means I know exactly what some words mean, but with most, I just have a general sense of how and where they might pop up, but can't really define them. I don't know what they mean when they stand naked before me, without a few nearby verbs, adjectives, or nouns to keep them company and give them context.

* * * * *

One night, my family rattled down the long, gravel driveway and into the dark, cold barnyard after a night out at a seafood restaurant on a nearby bay. We opened the car doors and were greeted with frigid air on which hovered the wailing of a phantom. It was coming from down below the paddocks, and it sounded like a six-foot-tall mourning dove lamenting a broken wing as it gradually died in the wet, cold grass.

"*Howooooo!*"

The sound filled me with dread. The sound was dread. It was the least earthly thing I'd ever heard, and it filled the vast, quiet night. It sounded intimate, like something you weren't supposed to hear.

If my mind were a cave, the source of this sound, this mortally wounded harpy or whatever it was, cast a vast, sorrowful shadow. I backed up to the car, placing my shoulder against the hard green metal of the passenger-side door.

"Let's go find out what that is," my dad said to a friend who was visiting from out of town. "It sounds like it's coming from near the train tracks."

They set off into the night, excited to plunge into the blackness, their dress shoes crunching on the gravel, their tan autumn jackets rustling as they swung their arms. The wailing continued, and I harbored a legitimate fear my dad and his friend were about to get disemboweled by a werewolf.

What they found was a very large, very old woman, lying on a shattered hip on a sheet of flagstone in her backyard, covered by an afghan of darkness through which specks of moonlight, their contours shaped by the leaves of overheard trees, illuminated her.

When my dad told us, I knew what came next. He was going to shoot her. This was a farm, after all, and I'd seen what happened to large mammals with broken legs. He was going to, as he usually phrased it, "put her down," which always made it sound, as he readied his gun, like he was only going to make a sardonic comment and reduce the heifer's self-esteem a few notches.

I was wrong. He called an ambulance and the EMTs hauled her away. She healed and lived for another 20 years, albeit with no monkeys and a creaky, irascible hip joint.

TANTRUMS

Sometimes my four-year-old daughter throws enormous temper tantrums. Giant, booming, Wagnerian operas of emotion, full of red-faced theatrics, simultaneously absurd and completely sincere.

I don't write about them often because, well, there are some things that you really can't put into words. Like being blown away in a Category 5 hurricane or being mauled by a grizzly bear while learning your identity was stolen and your car caught on fire, you can go on and on about how unpleasant it was, but you really have to live through it to fully understand.

On a side note, I just tried to Google "The worst type of hurricane" to remind myself how high the categories go. Before I could even type the "h," my browser saw what I was doing and tried to help me out, auto-filling with: "The worst type of cancer." It is 5 o'clock in the morning. Thanks, Internet.

I've read that tantrums are a natural part of growing up. That they are inevitable, and that we don't have the right to complain because we chose this life. Nobody wants to hear a skydiver go on and on about a little bit of windburn, or a clown gripe about the fact that he took a pie to the face. No one wants to see a matador lament about a couple of bleeding, horn-shaped holes in his thigh; no one forced him to put on his fanciest tights and his best Mickey Mouse ear hat and start taunting a 2,000-pound beast.

I chose this, so I shouldn't complain when my little girl bursts into tears, kicks, and proclaims this to be the "worst day ever" because I had the audacity to buy her vanilla ice cream, rather than the vanilla ice cream she had explicitly asked for five minutes earlier.

* * * * *

We recently spent nine days on a lake in New Hampshire. While my daughter and I swam and played, I sometimes stopped to chat with my wife, who does not swim. Inevitably, we debated whether or not swimming is one of those skills you can magically do if you are motivated strongly enough.

"Well, I can't swim," she always says. "But I could probably swim if I were drowning!"

"I don't think it works that way," I reply. "People can't suddenly fly if, and only if, they fall out of an airplane."

"Oh, I could probably do it if I really wanted to," she responded. "It's just that I don't enjoy it, so I don't want to try right now."

Several people have told me that swimming is a bit like riding a bike. "Once you know how to do it, you'll always know how!" they proclaim.

While treading water with the shoreline a fuzzy little panorama in the far distance, I suddenly realized that there are a couple key differences between cycling and swimming. For starters, if you do forget how to ride a bike, all you have to do is get off and walk. If you want to stop swimming in the middle of a lake or ocean, there is still the task of getting to shore.

The other thing I realized is that, sure, I will always remember HOW to swim, in much the same way that I know how to dunk a basketball (just jump really high), how to scale Mount Everest (climb really high and give all the heavy stuff to the guides), and how to win a Nobel Prize for Literature (just write a really great book). That said, to implement this knowledge, one must have things like muscle mass, endurance, or talent. I could easily sink to the bottom of the sea as my legs and arms grew too tired to obey, all the while thinking, "But I know HOW to swim. What's happening right now?"

Young children can build up muscle mass at an alarming rate. After a week in the water, little Hadley's legs were starting to bulge with new muscles, pulling the smooth, sandstone-colored skin taut over them. When she leapt up into my arms, bounding into the air so high that I worried she was about to take flight and join a passing flock of gulls, I imagined what one of her tantrums would be like if she were, you know, immensely physically powerful.

As she embraced me and whispered, "I love you, Daddy," I felt the frightening power in her arms as they closed around me, and I suddenly felt enormous empathy for John and Martha Kent. "What do you do when your child is an 'X-Man' and you bring her the wrong flavor ice cream?!" I wondered.

"You've been getting a lot of fresh air and exercise lately," I said. "Maybe it's time to sit in front of the television for a few hours." Maybe it's time for a little atrophy, just to level the playing field, I thought.

My fears—these particular fears, at least—are unfounded. She is getting stronger, but when she emerges from bed each morning, the thing I'm most struck by is just how small she really is. She's three feet tall! She weighs 35 pounds! She's like a hobbit.

As she wobbles out into the world each morning, rubbing the sleep from her eyes and telling me about the most wonderfully bizarre dreams, I'm always shocked by how very diminutive she really is.

It's the same way I feel when I meet celebrities in person. I hear the same thing from other people, too.

"Morgan Freeman was nice," they'll say. "He was smaller than I expected."

It's because the size of a person has nothing to do with the metaphysical space they take up, and the muscles in their little arms have nothing to do with their immense psychological power when you really, really love them.

Still, I wonder: How can someone who looms so large in my mind, someone whose sheer force of personality is so epic in scale, be no bigger than a plump raccoon? She has to look UP at door knobs! I realize this, reminded yet again that our world is one of contradictions, where things can hold several essential properties at once, both large and small, beautiful and ugly, despondent and hopeful.

DANDELIONS

I love dandelions.

Perhaps it's because they are my daughter's favorite flowers. The "little sunflowers" as she calls them, which she always picks and presents to me with the greatest reverence, like she is proud that such beauty can exist in the same world as her and I. With help from her mom, she knots them together to form a golden crown, and when she places it on my head, I really do feel like the emperor, if not of the world at least of my own little portion of it. I hold my head a little higher, knowing we are surrounded by beauty, and that I've done something right, because my daughter is not blind to it as so many others are.

Why do people hate some types of flowers, but spend billions of dollars trying to cultivate others? Why do they choose to rob themselves of time with their own families in a futile battle against a small plant that isn't hurting anyone? I doubt anyone, on their deathbed, ever said: "I wish I'd spent more time trying to rid the world of small yellow flowers."

Dandelions don't harm anyone or anything, my chickens eat them and they therefore save me money on feed, and they attract bees that pollinate fruit and other flowers. So dandelions are welcome in my yard. They are the least of my concerns, in a world that is admittedly filled with countless much more serious, much more grave things about which to worry.

Yet I regularly encounter seemingly nice people who tell me they "hate" dandelions. This is a word we tell our children not to use unless you are talking about the worst kind of monsters. Yet people fling it around wantonly, and sometimes they even do it in front of my four-year-old child, which makes me want to cover her ears.

"I hate dandelions," they say, and it seems like they might be virtue signaling, as if their hatred of a harmless little yellow flower is an indisputable sign of their good character.

"Why?" I always ask, genuinely curious.

"Because they are weeds!" people generally reply. But "weed" is simply a word people use to describe plants they hate. So what they are really saying is "I hate them because they are something I hate." It's maddeningly circular. It is hollow and completely devoid of logic, internal or external. Perhaps if you hate something—be it a type of person, or a food, or a variety of flower—and your only reason is that it is something you hate, you might be a bit too liberal with your application of hatred.

Does it follow that you love things only because they are things that you love? Nations and political parties and people? Or do you apply your love to things and people who actually deserve it?

I often feel alone, as I push my daughter on her swing-set and wonder if I'm just not seeing something that everyone else in suburban America sees. Is green grass really better than a bright yellow flower? If so, why?

But apparently I'm not completely alone.

"Let dandelions grow," read a headline in *The Guardian* newspaper. "Bees, beetles and birds need them."

"Dandelions are demonized as one of the most pernicious weeds, but hold back on the mowing and you'll find a whole range of garden wildlife depends on them for food," the article goes on to state.

This philosophy is not particularly new, either. Right around the time I was born, which is distressingly close to being synonymous with 40 years ago, the *New York Times* published the following: "This is the time of the dandelion, when its blossom brightens up or—depending on how one feels about it—messes up the lawn. Most people, who hold to a Calvinist notion that a weed-free lawn is a necessary way to grace, look on the dandelion as a weed to be sternly cast out. Others, who have a let-live philosophy of lawns, find that the happy color it adds to the grass in spring makes up for its shabby look the rest of the year."

But my soft spot for this flower probably lies in the sentence that comes next in the *Times* article: "The dandelion has many virtues and few defenders, though it has done well enough without them…"

Perhaps that's why I love the dandelion. Because it thrives, despite people's animosity toward it. Because it doesn't seem to care about all the hatred in the world, and its little golden flowers, which can adorn the most elegant of crowns, are like bursts of transcendent laughter in the face of all that is wrong.

GLUTEN-FREE JESUS

"**E**xcuse me, is this human meat gluten free?"

"Well, sir, that roast there, which is on sale by the way, is actually both 100 percent human and 100 percent divine..."

"Yeah, it says that on the sticker, but that doesn't really answer my question."

"...and it's also 100 percent ghost. I don't see the little 'gluten-free' symbol anywhere. You know, the one that shows a piece of wheat with a line going through it."

"OK. That's probably good enough. We try not to eat gluten in our family, but you have to live a little, some of the time. Really cut loose and go wild!"

"Mmmn."

"Oh, just one more question," adds the customer. "What kind of diet was this man—or god, or ghost, or whatever—on? Was it organic?"

"Well, he lived a couple thousand years before the invention of pesticides, so I think that's a pretty safe bet."

"And was he free-range?"

"Oh yeah, he walked all the way across the Middle East. I think he actually walked to Egypt. Very free-range. But, again, no official sticker, or anything like that."

"One last question: Was he killed in a humane way?"

At this, the man behind the counter would blush and adjust his collar, knowing he'd lost another sale. "Well, no, not really. He was, well, tortured, made to wear a crown of thorns, then nailed to a board. He was crucified, which means he most likely died by suffocation because the lungs don't inflate properly when you're hung like that."

* * * * *

I was lying awake late one night re-reading a book about a Swiss reformer named Huldrych Zwingli. Zwingli is an ancestor of mine, and I'm bitter that he's no longer a household name, while his rival, German reformer Martin Luther, is. The two beer-swilling scholars clashed over their respective beliefs around the Eucharist, the Christian sacrament in which bread and wine are offered as the ceremonial flesh and blood of Jesus Christ. According to Christian orthodoxy, a priest recites a special incantation to transform the food and drink, known to Christians as "transubstantiation."

In college, I wrote a research paper about Luther and Zwingli's merciless debate over transubstantiation, wrongly assuming that my descent from such obviously good theological stock would impress my professor enough that it alone would guarantee at least a passing grade.

Luther and Zwingli both wanted to reform the Catholic church. They wished to strip it of elements they saw as pedantic, ostentatious, and overly bureaucratic. If this were music, they wanted to go door-to-door playing bluegrass, rather than being part of a massive digital orchestra that performed in tandem with a 3D laser show.

But they got bogged down in a debate about transubstantiation. In the Gospel of John, Jesus shares bread and wine with his followers, stating, "This is my flesh, this is my blood." Zwingli interpreted it as a metaphor, arguing that the bread and wine symbolize Jesus' flesh and blood. He argued that, since Christ is fully human, and he resides in heaven, and fully human people can only be in one place at any given time, and heaven is presumably far away, he cannot be fully present in everyone's little church every Sunday morning. He also pointed out, and this is true, that if your church's bread and wine were transformed into meat and blood, you would probably be able to taste it.

So it was symbolic, not literal, in Zwingli's eyes.

Luther, like the Catholic church and most Christians at the time, thought Zwingli was insane. He contended that priests were actually able to literally transform bread and wine into flesh and blood. Luther called those who didn't believe the bread and wine were real flesh and blood "fanatics," and he likened his crusade against them to one against satanic forces. His opponents, he claimed, were dangerous, deluded, and had succumbed to an attack by the Devil.

My paper on Luther and Zwingli was a failure. My professor pointed out, again and again, that I had lazily inserted scattershot quotes from the supporting texts, rather than laying out any discernible thesis. Whether Jesus was really there in the bread and wine would remain a mystery, he pointed out, but it was clear that a coherent argument was completely absent from my work, and that was clear, in a very literal way. It was a common theme when professors critiqued my writing.

I learned from the transubstantiation controversy, though. Primarily, it was a clear illustration of how incredibly bad people are at getting along.

Over the years, the issue faded to the recesses of my mind. The bread I ate grew darker, crustier, and was eventually full of ancient, heirloom grains that reached the pinnacle of their popularity around the time the New Testament was written. My wine changed, too. It got older, and it usually came in more svelte bottles adorned by fancy labels. My wine and my jelly are no longer derived from the exact same varietal of grape.

From time to time, my theological studies resurface. They're useful in daily life far more often than you'd expect. They open the world around me, working like mental paint thinner that instantly strips away the false façades with which we shellac our daily lives. A reality TV show about remodeling houses? Those people will get to sit on better couches and look at more soothing wallpaper while they worry about and wait for death.

The "gluten-free" Eucharist crackers I found for sale online? They are, apparently, all the rage, because many thousands of people have set aside the heated debate about whether or not the Eucharist really contains the flesh and blood of a God-Man, to talk about the literal presence of wheat.

But if Luther was right, and a magical incantation can transform these things, can't the priest just add an extra sentence to the spell, something about banishing any grain proteins that give some people gas or diarrhea? If they can turn bread into human meat, and if they can magically transform rock music into something really, deeply terrible, can't Christian leaders take a moment to help out the small number of people who are literally allergic to gluten, and the several million people who think they are?

That's not the right way to say it, I realize. They aren't imagining they can't digest wheat. They really can't, symbolically speaking, of course.

Eating human flesh is often frowned upon outside of church. But we do eat a lot of chicken. That's why I recently suggested to a group of friends that perhaps sustainable cockfighting might be the next big thing. Hipsters have opened shops (I think they spell it "shoppes") selling ice cream made from human breast milk and beer brewed with beard yeast, so it's not exactly an impossible idea. They would probably make it sustainable by eating the loser, making it a "green," slightly ironic form of screen-free entertainment.

At this point, an old friend of mine emerged from a bundle of striped scarf and waved his hand in disgust. He found my suggestion appalling.

"No!" he shouted. "I want to eat a champion."

"What?"

"I don't want to eat losers," he explained. "I'm the kind of guy who eats winners."

He got me thinking. Food plays an enormous role in most religions. Along with talk of demons and angels and gods, there are always instructions about what people can and cannot eat, and when. I think it's because religion is not bound by any of the rules that govern the rest of the things in our lives. Religion, by definition, has no parameters. It's the one place where people can fly, rise from the dead, and even feed their hungry souls with stories that are rich in metaphysical calories despite lacking physical matter.

People need souls, so they invent them. They dream up their souls, their souls need spiritual nourishment, so they have to dream that up, too. I have a good friend with whom I debate this issue every day, usually on the phone, for about an hour, while we clean up after our respective daughters or drive to and from work. He thinks it's all a bunch of nonsense. It's merely an invention.

I disagree. Religion is an invention. Just like the twin ideas of love and justice. Just like pizza. Just like stained glass. Just like music. It's something we made up, and now we can't live without it. It's the thing that makes our species unique; we're narrative alchemists. We can make stories out of nothing, and those stories are so good that we need them, like oxygen or water. We can invent things that are essential to our lives. We need beauty in order to live, and so, of course, we make it.

We need them because God is an idea always in the corner of your eye. If you look directly at it, it vanishes. Even when you know the stories aren't literally true, you also know they only work if you tell them as if they are. There are ancient people who believe that the next world is like this one, only harder, and that it wears you down until your feet, your legs, and all the rest of you have been erased.

When the last bit of you is gone, you are born back into this world, to walk again on the soft grass.

Trees are known by their fruits, and God is the ripest fruit of humanity. A sacred baby conceived of and cared for by billions of everyday people. It is both imagined and real. Things really can be both.

A LOVE TAIL

All rodent-based fashion trends are doomed to failure in the end. I should know, because I used to have a tail.

A "rat tail."

It began when I saw fourth-grade girls ogling Jordan, a guy in a band called New Kids on the Block. He seemed incredibly lame, to revert to the parlance of the late 1980s, and he sang syrupy pop songs like a child in a medieval church choir, but every girl in school adored him.

Love is that easy when you're nine years old. You don't have to maintain a romantic bond with someone while you share a home, change diapers, and make sure you pay all your bills only a few days late each month. All you have to do is declare it, like it's a box of heart-shaped chocolates you're trying to bring through customs.

They declared it with gusto. They loved him. But love is one of those terms that embraces all sorts of meanings in many different times and places.

I didn't know much about love back then, and I hypothesized that the long, sometimes-braided strip of hair that hung down Jordan's neck—which, combined with the poofy, product-laden hair on top of his head looked very much like the tail of a marmot that had climbed onto his scalp—was the secret. So I grew one. Maybe, if my hair looked like his, I too could be loved.

Perhaps the ridiculous strip of hair was like some magical talisman, I thought. Maybe he was like Samson, if Samson wore high-top shoes with the laces hazardously but stylishly untied.

It took a year. By fifth grade, I had a nice—another word with a loose, malleable meaning when used here—rat tail running down my neck. It reached its peak at the precise moment the nation's love affair with the New Kids On the Block came to a spontaneous, universal end. All the love — an emotion packed with meaning and energy—couldn't just evaporate, but it could not stay love forever. So it did what fickle affection usually does; it transformed into equally passionate loathing. Right around the same time, the popularity of rat tails came to a sudden and calamitous end.

Yet for one brief moment, my tail had its desired effect. In homeroom, I was seated directly in front of a tall, passionate, physically powerful (this part comes up again later) girl, whom we'll call Lynn here so she does not seek me out and rough me up (again). Even at that young age, you could tell she would one day look like a supermodel.

Lynn fell deeply in love with me and my tail, filling my desk to the brim with love notes that were, in retrospect, full of troubling, fairly heavy-handed foreshadowing. The general theme was that she had to have me, and if she didn't, she would simply have to light the entire world on fire instead.

I was instructed by my friends, people who could barely tie their own shoelaces, to play "hard to get." So I played it aloof.

"Did you get my note?" she'd ask of a 1,000-word poem.

"Yup," I'd reply. "See ya."

If I ignored her in class, she would yank on my tail. It's a remarkably effective way to redirect someone's gaze. It's also quite painful, which, combined with the fact that it makes you look utterly hideous, is probably one of the reasons you don't see a lot of rat tails today.

She chased me endlessly on the playground. One day, I scaled the monkey bars with her in dogged pursuit. When I reached the top, there was nowhere to go but down. I was like the hero of an action movie, backed up against a cliff. As she approached, preparing to bury me beneath a deluge of kisses, I turned, took a deep breath, and jumped. In midair, I unexpectedly paused—not figuratively, but literally —as a very strong hand held the weight of my body aloft, and I dangled from a little thicket of hair that jutted out from the back of my neck.

She had me by the tail, and she wouldn't let go. It lasted only a second. Then, to my simultaneous relief and chagrin, a large clump of hair came free from my neck, and I plummeted to the hard earth below. Rolling over and gazing up, I saw Lynn standing atop the monkey bars, searing white rays of midday sun pouring around her tall frame and through the scraggly clump of liberated hair she held in her fist.

She was beautiful. There was no debating it, seeing her up there like that. That night, I stayed up late, laboring over a love letter. In it, I told her I'd been a fool to play hard-to-get. I told her I loved her too, although I stopped short of vowing to set fire to anyone or anything should things not work out in the end. I guess I'm just not that much of a romantic.

The next day, I slipped it into her desk. After school, one of her friends approached me with a message.

"She's over you," she said. "She doesn't love you anymore."

Today, I love my wife. The notes we write to one another are not messages of unbridled passion, but rather utilitarian communications about what time to pick up our three-year-old daughter, or whether or not the dog ate chocolate, then got diarrhea all over the floor. She doesn't pull my hair, and I don't tempt her by growing it into a tail. Fashion trends may come and go, but this kind of love, I know, will last forever.

EVERYDAY WEIRD

You excuse yourself from the restaurant table around which you've gathered with friends and stroll through the big, cacophonous overload of background chatter and dim lights. Then something beautiful happens when you enter the bathroom.

You step through the door, and as it swings shut behind you, the din outside drops to a hushed whisper. The lavatory lighting is higher than it was outside, and it is relentlessly white or blue or yellow. The lights hum their unassuming little song. There is an echo and an absence of movement. The surfaces are hard and nonporous. The lighting always blinds you for a moment. When your vision returns, you find yourself draped in bright light, gazing at a vent, or a tile, or a rusty hinge, or a plumbing fixture, or a single letter in a line of graffiti scrawled on the wall.

During these moments, I experience a Russian literary phenomenon called *ostranenie*. You gaze at a stall door hinge, which functions as a makeshift coat hanger and looks like a face.

You stand at the urinal and begin to study the wisdom left behind by those who preceded you. Staring at some tactless carnal overture authored by someone who plays fast and loose with tense and capitalization, you think: "What on earth? Is that what the letter "G" looks like? What a bizarre symbol. Have I not seen a "G" before? That's not possible, is it?"

It's the same thing that happens when you look at a common word for long enough, a word you've written and read hundreds of thousands of times: "Is that how you spell the word 'roof'?!" you think with alarm as it breaks down to its component parts and reassembles in a new way.

You are stuck, motionless, and you see a ceiling fan or a paper towel as if for the very first time. And you wonder, "How have I lived for 30 years without ever really looking at these things that inhabit the world?!"

These are some of the funniest, most beautiful things I've ever seen. And I've seen a man get kicked in the groin by a camel, so my bar for funny and beautiful is really incredibly high.

Because there is no English equivalent to *ostranenie*, translations vary. The word first appears in a 1917 essay called *Art as Device*. It has been translated as "defamiliarization" and also "making it strange." Personally, I associate author Anton Chekhov with *ostranenie*, defined by Chekhov biographer Thomas Winner as "a peculiar semantic shift which transfers a depicted object to a different plane of reality. The habitual is 'made strange' by a distortion, causing the perceiver to see the object in a fresh light, as though for the first time."

Experiencing this in the bathroom, I realize it's my working definition of humor, and I think it's no mistake that Chekhov insisted on calling many of his works—even ones that at first glance appear dreary or melancholy—comedies.

Scholar David Plante says Chekhov knew a coherent view of the world is impossible, and he therefore abandoned any attempt at one. Unable to see the world under the aspect of generalization, he instead presented it to his readers in its particulars, "and therefore his attention to the most vivid—and in their vividness the strangest—details."

If you really, really look at the things around you, you will find that they are all weird.

I think helping people see better—see themselves, see the world around them—is the point of all writing, or at least all literary writing. It follows that literary writing will usually be funny.

Why *ostranenie* can be so jarring is that we have forgotten the world is real. We get so wound up in our visceral responses to things, and we rely so heavily on the shortcuts we use to save time in our everyday lives, that we can go days, months, in the most tragic instances even entire lives, without really seeing the things and people around us as anything other than slightly out of focus props in a banal story whose protagonist is supremely unobservant.

Without looking down, what type of chair are you sitting in? What color is it? How are its legs affixed to the seat? Do the screws holding it together make scowling faces, or do they spell out some kind of exotic code or landscape? But you probably didn't inspect the chair. You saw something that looked chair-ish out of the corner of your eye, categorized it as such, with the million other chairs you've seen, and plopped down in it. You never really saw it.

Various things can help us achieve *ostranenie*. If you don't want to go to the trouble of reading Chekhov, you can always just reproduce. Spending time with a baby or small child throws trees, shoes, shopping carts, and silverware into the light of profundity. It makes everything fresh and new, and therefore strange, which is one of the standard definitions of "funny." Have you ever really looked at a shoe?

Even the simple act of getting down on the floor, to a baby's level, will show you that, while the real world is still there, it looks very different than you thought.

When my daughter was three, she somehow managed to unlock my iPhone, which I am humbled to point out is something I have not fully mastered. She opened the camera app, then roamed our house, clicking away. When, several days later, I came across the 30-some photos she took that day, I was astounded. It took me about a dozen to even recognize it as my own home.

I had never seen that coffee table before. That corner leading into the kitchen, with the little handprints on it. The knobs on the various cabinets, with their exuberant faces. The dusty underbelly of our family's home. The dog was photographed from below, his wrinkly black lips dripping down toward the camera.

"Whose dog is that?" I wondered for a second.

And of course, he isn't my dog. Not really. He is a dog who exists independently from me, in a world that is real, and strange, and rarely observed by those who amble through it. He, like me, and like my daughter, does not belong to me—he belongs to life's yearning for itself.

There are two very special ways of seeing something: the first time you see something, and the last. I've heard it said that one never truly sees anything until they see it for the last time. A sunset. A lover's face. The strange geography of your own hand.

This is why what writing does is so special. That is what books give us; to read is to re-see something for the first time, but well before the last.

PILLOW MEN

When Peter the Great returned to Russia after touring western Europe in the late 17th century, he wanted his citizens to look more modern, so he created a law requiring men to shave their beards unless they paid a tax. Those who treasured their facial hair enough to pay the "beard tax" received a special medallion, which they had to carry at all times. Men who flouted the law risked having their beards forcibly removed by government officials in the streets.

Were I to run for public office, the beard tax would be a central component of my platform. Spin would be vital to its success, of course. A beard tax, if subtly rebranded as a "hipster fee," would be a rare kind of taxation that meets with nearly universal acclaim. People would continue bickering over funding for schools and highways, but the left and the right could finally unite over the justice of taking punitive fiduciary action against anyone whose entire personality is based upon the concept of vacuous aesthetic irony.

A skinny jeans tax might be a better vehicle for this, however, as it wouldn't have the unintended and unfortunate side effect of being effectively a weak chin tax, which I worry would be the kind of taxation, like an erectile dysfunction tariff or a diarrhea fee, that simply kicks people when they are already down.

I'm not opposed to interesting facial hair. After all, beards and mustaches used to be far more exciting. Just like everything else. That's why the nonchalance with which people lived their lives in the distant past amazes me. Things were insane, yet everyone thought it was normal, primarily because it was normal, at least back then. Because we are each entrenched in our own times and places.

"I'm going to climb on top of this 1,000-pound, marginally domesticated ungulate—the one over there with the flaring nostrils and eyeballs bulging with fear—the one that could kill me by kicking me, or stepping on me, or biting me, or by my simply falling off of it, and then I'm going to try to balance on its back for several hundred miles," the olden-times person would say.

"I see. And to where will you go?"

"I'm traveling to another country, the one with a doctor in it," he would reply. "I'm hoping he can cure me of my typhoid. And of whatever broken limbs I sustain during the ride there, obviously."

"Excellent. And have they found a cure for typhoid yet?"

"No, no. I'd better be off. Tell my wife and children I'll likely be gone a year or two, assuming all goes well."

When I look back, I find it difficult to believe just how exciting those times were. I read about someone dying from galloping dysentery, alabaster fever, or weasel pox, and I just think, "Yes, please!"

The most tragic thing about it, of course, is that people didn't even realize or appreciate that they were living inside a glorious adventure story back then. They thought every-thing was normal. Pirates and cowboys and knights and knaves and pharaohs. To them, it was all banal, all the time. They all dreamed of living in some alien time and place.

In the court of Peter the Great, a trained bear approached visitors while balancing a large glass of peppered brandy between its claw-studded paws. If they did not drink it, the bear was trained to rip off their clothes. This was the tsar's court, a place of high culture. These were people who went to the ballet for fun.

I, regretfully, have been unable to train a bear to do this. Honestly, I haven't even been able to get a trained bear. Or even a disobedient bear, for that matter. God knows I've tried. Plus, my wife insists that social mores have changed, and having a dangerous animal assault your friends is frowned upon in society today. Just another example of political correctness run amok, I guess.

It's because of the bear thing that I'm discernibly glum as I approach guests in my home, handing them a cup of warm chamomile tea. "I'm sorry," I say sheepishly. "This interaction would have been far more interesting in the time of Peter the Great. For starters, this would be brandy rather than tea, and, well, there would be other differences too."

Virtually everything was more interesting in Peter the Great's world. That, at least, was my takeaway when I read Robert Massie's Pulitzer-winning biography of the iconic Russian tsar. It is a revelation I found alarming—the possibility that I live in a leaden and dull time.

I fret when I think humanity had a finite amount of dynamism, and that we already mined and burned most of it 300 years ago in a cold, faraway land where buildings look like colorfully-painted onions.

Gone are the days of dwarf parades, public torture parties, and pillow men. What's a pillow man? Peter the Great always used a pillow man when he was out on military campaigns.

This was a different time in world history. Great leaders were known to have wacky tastes and unique fetishes. Ibrahim the Mad, a grand vizier and contemporary of Peter, found the most heightened state of sexual rapture in the arms of large women—he reasoned that if a little woman could give X amount of gratification, one twice her size would be able to offer twice as much. I'm not great at math, but there is a certain internal logic at play, you have to admit.

Ibrahim, who rarely left his palace, festooned his beard with priceless jewels, and wished to feel only elegant furs against his skin when not in the squishy embrace of a hefty woman, sent out his best agents to find and bring back the fattest woman in all the land. It's a nice twist on a traditional Disney fairy tale.

Peter's interest in pillow men was not sexual. He simply found that in a tent, in the middle of the muddy, icy Russian wilderness, the most comfortable object upon which to rest his head was a warm, soft, human stomach. After a long day expanding the largest empire on earth, he would call for a pillow man, lay his head on the pillow man's belly, and soon fall fast asleep.

It was, apparently, a landscape where nothing was soft except for people. And people, Ibrahim's girlfriends notwithstanding, aren't even really that soft.

While the historical record provides little information about these key figures in the making of modern Russia, my friends and I have been able—through a combination of extensive conjecture, and also more conjecture—to fill in the gaps.

Human bedding must be soft, and Peter's head would have been uncomfortable on a flat, firm stomach. Likewise, it would have simply rolled off of one that was overly bloated. A pillow man must never do sit-ups, and he must never ingest foods that would lead to gaseous buildup in his lower intestine. No trips to the gym, and no boiled cabbage.

Pillow men would have been among the most trustworthy people in the tsar's court, since a pillow man would be in a unique position to assassinate his ruler. They would also be a good last defense against would-be assassins, who would slink into the tent in the dead of night, try to grab a pillow with which to smother the sleeping tsar, and utter something along the lines of, "Oh wait, this pillow is actually a guy!"

Perhaps, we hypothesized, some of the better ones came from a long line of pillow men. Like a blacksmith or a knight. Maybe, like people named "Shepard," "Smith," or "Mason," they would even end up with a surname indicative of their family trade. Maybe there's some guy walking around in Ohio today named "Jeff Pillowman," who knows nothing of the vital role his ancestors played in world history.

Sadly, good pillow men are very difficult to find these days. I think they might even be extinct.

It's yet another reminder that most of Peter the Great's world is gone forever. Even his dynasty is gone. It ended in the middle of the night, many generations after Peter's death, when Tsar Nicholas II, his wife, their three innocent daughters, and their hemophiliac son were led into a cold, cramped basement, told they were about to be photographed, then cut down in a flurry of bullets that ripped most of the plaster from the walls and much of the flesh from their bodies.

According to eyewitnesses, Nicholas' final words were: "What? What?" That means he was confused, and not even particularly original in the way he expressed it.

* * * * *

Peter is gone, but as long as I'm around, not forgotten.

My interest in Peter the Great is intense and enjoyable. But, like the month I ate only Indian food or the summer I bought a canoe and tried to become a river pirate, it seemed destined to fizzle out of its own volition.

Then a man moved into the house next door to ours. He's from Russia, and, looking to move somewhere warmer, chose to settle in the American Midwest. His name is Vlad, which seems almost redundant, like an American named "Tex."

I spent the first year of our friendship suffering obediently through conversations about our children and the weather so I could get to the topics I really wanted to cover. "What was your childhood in Russia like?" "When you were a kid, did a pet bear bring you your brandy to drink, or did you have to get your own drinks?"

At first, he swore his childhood was just like any other, except with more bread lines. Then, as time went on and we became closer, he would, from time to time, let slip little gems of information, seemingly unaware of how exotic they sounded to me. I've always been a sucker for the "other," and to me, "different" and "weird" are merely synonyms for "good." I know Russia has impressive centers of metropolitan refinement, but my friend didn't grow up in them. He grew up in their version of Arkansas.

He even discovered a Russian grocery store nearby. At first, the owners, a young couple who had come to America a decade ago, seemed suspicious of me. Much to my surprise, they didn't even want to talk about Peter the Great. A friend suggested that perhaps my attempts to discuss their long-dead tsar were like a Japanese woman approaching me on the street and asking if I had strong feelings about the policies enacted by former U.S. President Millard Fillmore.

At the Russian store, I browse the aisles and buy containers whose labels are covered with the Cyrillic alphabet. It might as well be Martian to me. When I get home, I enjoy the surprise of opening—and sometimes even eating—whatever I find inside. Most contain pickles. One could, without risking a major rebrand, simply start calling the Russian grocery store "the Pickle Store." Sometimes I find I've purchased sprats, which are little, fatty, black and silver fish that come smoked and meticulously arranged in circular black and gold tins. They taste like slices of butter that have been fermented at the bottom of a salty and ancient sea.

When my daughter was first learning to speak, my wife came into the room to find her eating a plate full of these small sea creatures. We'd been talking, little Hadley and I, about just how interesting the world has the ability to be.

She'd been alive for only two years, and she had already flown through the sky, looking down at the earth from 40,000 feet. She had seen Shakespeare performed, and she had been cured of and vaccinated against several diseases that used to extinguish entire civilizations in a matter of months. She had heard the voice of Orson Welles, who died many years before she was born, on the radio, and she had watched Charlie Chaplin dance with a stray dog in his pants, even though he too is rotting in the ground.

She is familiar with numbers and letters, which means she will be able to decipher a lifetime of beautiful codes and ciphers, from love letters and novels to birth announcements, and obituaries, and books full of funny little stories. She talks to her cousins, who live in a far, far away land, through a vivid, magical screen, and she has even climbed atop a small, semi-domesticated ungulate, which was old and quite docile and quite possibly teetering on the very brink of its own mortality, and ridden around in a few blissful circles.

She lives, I know and appreciate, in a time full of nearly limitless adventure and opportunity.

A few days later, she fell asleep one afternoon with her head on my stomach. I was pinned, and I couldn't even reach a book to read, or a video game controller to fiddle with. So I stayed there, motionless, for an hour and a half, until she awoke naturally from her nap. One of my arms was asleep, and my neck would be stiff for a couple days. But it's all just part of the job. All just part of being a parent.

All just part of being a pillow man.

MEH, NOT SO FUNNY

A good review can be good, but only a bad review can achieve greatness.

More than any other species, our very nature, and even the reality of our existence, is based upon how each individual experiences the world. Cows don't wander around wondering if they exist, whether God exists, whether beauty exists, or whether the existence of any of them is contingent upon the ability to conceive of them. But we do. I do, at least.

That's why people often put the word "arguably" before claims about greatness, as a qualifier. It's just a small admission that yes, each person's value judgments are unique. That's why the Beatles are "arguably" the greatest band ever, and *War and Peace* is "arguably" the best book. Because everything is arguable. If you don't believe me, just look at the comment section below the least controversial thing you can imagine on YouTube—a sick kid petting a puppy, or something—and notice how quickly it becomes a rancorous debate about Trump or whether or not 9/11 was an inside job.

At the beginning of *Swann's Way*, Marcel Proust talks about the experience of waking up in his bedroom as a child. For a moment, he lies there as a mere husk, ignorant of the world and even of himself. Then, his past experiences —the places he has been and might currently be—come flooding back into his mind. When this is over, he is once again himself.

We've probably all experienced this. The fleeting moment of bliss the morning after a loved one dies, before you remember the reality into which you are opening your eyes. One might argue that the world is there, but 100 percent of what we know of the world around us, of our children and our gods and our friends, is gathered and understood through our subjective experiences.

Proust even wonders if maybe the only thing that holds the doorknob and the lamp to their forms and functions as doorknobs and lamps, is the very fact that we conceive them as such. And I wonder if religion isn't just the idea that maybe, our forms and functions are the way they are because something else conceives us to be that way.

Whenever this gets me down, whenever I fret because millions of people think the world is flat, or whatever, I can always make myself feel better by reading bad reviews of things I know to be the pinnacle of human achievement. You don't have to go far. Amazon and Goodreads are home to thousands of one-star reviews of the very best books ever written, arguably.

James Joyce's *Ulysses* has about a thousand one-star reviews on Goodreads. One reviewer explained his low rating this way: "It fell in my toilet and I'm accepting it as an act of god."

The one-star reviews of Isabel Allende's elegant *The House of the Spirits* are particularly fun. One states simply:

"I think this book was alright but there is a lot of confusing things." Indeed.

Another says he hated the book, then admits he didn't actually read it. One reviewer, who also gave it one star and also admitted she had not actually read the whole book, said she didn't like it because someone was mean to a chicken in it.

Boring one-star reviews tend to run screaming into the realm of politics. "This is communist propaganda!" is a popular trope.

Good ones push the boundaries of what a review is, and what it can tell us about ourselves.

Critics of humorous prose have it easy. All they really have to say is "not funny" and their work is pretty much done. After all, humor is even more subjective than most things. But David Sedaris might be the most clever author on the planet. And his tales of love and woe reach deep into our collective souls. Thousands of people disagree with me, apparently.

One reviewer of his *Me Talk Pretty One Day* even penned her one-star review directly to the author, as if in the hopes that maybe she could convince him to stop writing: "You think you're funny? Meh, not that funny. Special? You're not that special either. You're a writer, just another writer. What's the big deal?"

Another critic said she was "appalled" by the book: "[In my opinion], his joke regarding his pet's need for dialysis was especially scathing since I lost my beloved 18-year-old shih tzu to chronic kidney failure last year." Her profile photo is of her with a little dog, probably before its demise. She shelved the book in a couple categories, including "books set in New York" and "worst books I've ever read."

I really love all dogs, and I really love some humans, even writers like Mr. Sedaris. I think it's possible to love them both. I'd like to point out that this person's shih tzu was 126 in dog years when it died, which seems like something short of a tragedy.

Cruelty to animals does seem to produce bad reviews. Perhaps I should delete the part, in my next manuscript, where I kick an endangered panda to death, or the entire chapter where I discuss the best ways to light a chipmunk on fire.

Yet another reader is more diplomatic in her review of Sedaris. She writes, simply: "I didn't think it was funny. Is something wrong with me?"

Yes.

My favorite bad review is for *The Collected Works of William Shakespeare*. Surely, you think, this book receives only five-star reviews and glowing praise, right? I mean, it's SHAKESPEARE.

This one comes from Amazon. These reviews are notorious among authors, because people often give poor ratings based on the amount of time the book took to arrive in the mail, or whether or not the pages of a used copy were dog-eared, two things that not even the best author can really control.

This review is so wonderful I took a screenshot of it, so I can look at it whenever I feel low.

The Collected Works of William Shakespeare received a damning single star. The reason? The reviewer, who I'll admit is more to the point than the Bard, explains it in a single sentence:

"I didn't order this."

Fair enough.

AFTERBIRTH

When we came home from the hospital after my wife gave birth, we buried something deep in the backyard, underneath a blueberry bush. Then the bush withered and died.

It began at a prenatal trip to the doctor.

"What do you plan to do with the placenta?" he asked.

I had no idea. I didn't even know what the options were, let alone which one to select.

"Leave it in?"

"Remove it?"

"Test it... for something?"

"Feed it... to...someone?"

They all ran through my mind, but I wasn't confident enough to say any of them aloud.

To be honest, I barely knew what I planned to do with the baby, let alone the slime that trailed behind her. I hadn't even known what to do with myself for most of the prior three decades. When in doubt, I tended to just get good and drunk. But afterbirth isn't sentient, so beer would be wasted on it. And while babies probably can get hammered, I'm not firmly convinced they should.

"That's a good question," I answered, buying time.

If I had the power to see the future, I would have answered with confidence: "We're going to bring it home in a Tupperware container, bury it in the ground in the backyard, plant a blueberry bush on top of it, then feel incredibly guilty when the plant dies."

But the future was murky, as always, so I remained silent. "Throw it in the trash!" felt like the wrong thing to say about something so closely linked to our baby.

As with everything else around childbirth, I suspected I'd give the wrong answer and my baby would be confiscated by the state when she came out. Adopting a stray cat involves a delicate and treacherous bureaucratic dance, and I've even had someone refuse to remit a puppy into my custody before. Being denied a human was never far from my mind. It seemed like a real and embarrassing possibility.

Doctors and nurses, aunts and uncles—they all kept asking how prepared we were. What year was our car-seat made? Did we have an appropriate system of weights, pulleys, and stanchions to prevent me from rolling over onto our daughter while I slumbered? Did we plan to pollute the environment with disposable diapers, or would we give the earth a break by allowing our beloved offspring to wallow in her own filth?

I answered all those and more, but I didn't have the parameters or knowledge to confront the afterbirth query. My wife, weary from being poked, prodded, and smeared with cold, translucent sonogram jelly, looked to me, as if we'd been asked if we were planning to perform the birthing ceremony in Esperanto or not. She bobbed her head impatiently in the direction of the doctor, as if to say, "Answer him!"

It seemed like a fair deal. She'd grow the baby in her womb for nine months, then endure excruciating pain for 30 hours in order to deliver it safely into the world. All I was being asked to do was answer a couple questions from a doctor.

I started talking and listened to see how it went. It's an admittedly white-knuckle conversational technique.

"When I was a kid, my dog liked to eat the cows' afterbirth. But he only got it if the mother cow didn't eat it first," I began, a little cautiously. I studied the doctor's face carefully while I spoke, looking for a nod of approval, perhaps even some agreement. Something to indicate I was on the right narrative track.

What I saw was something more akin to confusion, so I deftly altered my course: "But we don't have any cows. We live in town. We have a dog. I guess that's not really relevant?"

Our doctor had an odd rhetorical quirk: He began nearly every sentence by saying, "I'm not going to lie to you…"

It didn't matter what came next.

"I'm not going to lie to you," he'd say. "Your next checkup is on the 24th."

Or: "I'm not going to lie to you. Your baby's heart sounds just fine."

He was seeking our trust too hard, which of course made me want to withhold it. Plus, on the rare occasions he didn't start a sentence that way, I automatically assumed he was lying.

"What do you suggest we do with the placenta, Doctor?" I asked.

"I'm not going to lie to you," he replied. "People do all sorts of things with it."

In doctors, I prefer precise, crisp language. Vagaries often lead to unnecessary problems in the operating room, I imagine. "We got your biopsy results," the imprecise doctor might report. "They show all sorts of things!"

Luckily, ours did provide details. "Some new parents bury the placenta in the backyard and plant a tree or shrub on top of it," he said.

"That," my wife said, the perimeter of her voice tinted with fatigue. "We're going to do that." There was no need to hear other options.

We brought it home, plopped into a plastic container, and planted it in the backyard. I dug a deep hole, dropping the liver-colored blob into it, covered it with black soil, and planted a beautiful little blueberry bush, which almost immediately withered and died, to mark the spot.

That, in case Big Brother is reading this, is why my Internet search history includes the following query: "Blueberry bush on wife's placenta died! Is baby sick?"

Turns out, blueberries don't grow in the part of Wisconsin where we live. It has something to do with the acidity levels in the soil. It was a troubling omen, nonetheless.

We'd chosen a blueberry because that's what we had called our unborn daughter in the prenatal months leading up to her birth. We followed a blog that told us, in increasingly confusing ways, what size she was each week. The first week we looked it up, the blog told us she was the size of a blueberry. The name stuck, at least until we found a permanent replacement.

As the weeks progressed, the fruit used as examples became increasingly obscure. I didn't even know there were 36 different types of fruit, let alone fruit to perfectly represent the size of a growing fetus at regular intervals for three trimesters. When I learned she was the size of a grape, I nodded in understanding. The same went for an orange. But a jackfruit? The information was of no use to me. Plus, I envisioned her taking on all the characteristics of each fruit, not just the size. One week she was a lumpy yellow gourd, the next she was a leaden, green, perfectly round melon. The pineapple week, I kept thinking, must have been hell for my wife. Plus, we eat a lot of heirloom fruits and vegetables, and the sizes vary. A lot. Sometimes a tomato is larger than a head of cabbage. One week she was an eggplant, we learned.

"The Korean kind?" my wife asked.

"I don't know," I admitted.

When the delivery finally happened, I was slightly surprised my wife didn't give birth to a decorative fruit basket.

One day, a year or so later, while at a friend's house, I watched as he reached into a large chest freezer. He was selecting which cut of meat to thaw for dinner that night. "Whoops, don't want to cook that one," he muttered. "That's our placenta. We tossed it in here and then forgot about it."

"I'm not going to lie to you," I responded. "Ours is in the yard, buried underneath a dead blueberry bush."

It's a reminder of life, and death, and dirt, and love and loss, and how very closely linked all those things are. That way I won't forget that life is messy, and short, and we all weaken and die. Knowing that, we hold our loved ones closer, and with more tenderness, and we know that is what to do with our lives.

THE LOON

"Woman Chokes Bobcat to Death."

"And I'll take one of those," I said to the convenience store clerk, pointing to a newspaper where I saw the headline. "Please."

I was in New Hampshire, on vacation, and I wanted to get a sense of the local culture by reading regional news. Apparently, I had chosen to unwind and relax in a place where middle-aged women sometimes kill wild animals with their bare hands.

"Well-behaved women rarely make history," read the bumper sticker a 46-year-old local woman was affixing to her rear bumper when the wild cat pounced. According to the article, predator and prey became gripped in a death match she was certain to lose.

But that isn't what happened.

Somehow the woman was able to bring her hands down around the animal's neck and choke the life right out of it. When her son arrived with a knife, he killed it some more.

With the cat dead, the loons that inhabit the nearby lake where we were staying were surely breathing a sigh of relief.

I had recently turned 39, and until last week I had only heard the word "loon" used in one manner. If you look it up in the *American Heritage Dictionary*, one of the definitions of a "loon" is "one who is crazy or simple-minded."

Apparently there is a second definition: "A diving bird with mottled plumage and an eerie, laugh-like cry."

I wasn't really asking to learn all about loons; I was doing pretty well without them, but that didn't stop everyone in New Hampshire from teaching me about them. My mother, who lives there, has chosen it as a kind of totem animal that adorns paintings, paperweights, dishes, and even the inspirational signs that are nailed to every wall in her home.

These signs give me lots of unsolicited advice about how to lead a meaningful and virtuous life. They always sound good, but they are inevitably impossible to apply. Things like, "If you stumble, make it part of the dance!" The slogans stare at me while I wash my hands or make a sandwich, and I always stare back, thinking how unsettling it would be to see someone trip and fall, then get up and start doing a wild, interpretive dance routine.

No thanks. If I fall, I think I'll just admit it was an accident, dust myself off, and keep walking. Which brings me back to loons, which can fly elegantly through the sky and glide majestically across the black surface of a cold, dark, evergreen-scented northern lake. But they cannot walk, because their legs are positioned too far back, perilously far from their center of gravity. Once I learned this, I wanted only one thing: to see a loon accidentally wind up on land, so I could see it trying to walk. If it really couldn't, I'd go over and help, nudging it into the water.

But first I'd offer a little advice as the bird flopped around on the ground, emitting an eerie cry and kicking up pine needles.

"If you stumble," I'd say. "Make it part of the dance!"

JOHN UPDIKE

The dung pile sat steaming on John Updike's lawn. A black mountain of former life and future potentiality—a fecal exercise in reincarnation—freshly dumped onto the grass in front of a stately seaside manor.

Updike strolled down from his home, a heavily cabled, cream-colored sailor's sweater crawling up his neck and protecting his torso while his floppy, white hair bore the full brunt of the sea's cold, violent, and erratic exhalations. A little droplet of translucent moisture trembled from the underside of his nose, which was shaped like a pleasantly askew owl's beak.

My dad, standing face to face with him, pulled a handkerchief from his pocket. For a moment, I was terrified he was about to offer it to the famous writer, but instead he simply wiped away a tear the icy wind had called forth from the corner of his own eye. They were both leaking, it appeared. The Pulitzer Prize-winning author and the man who sold vintage cow manure for a living.

I knew my dad's eye often wept, but the fact that famous writers produced boogers was somehow surprising to me. I suddenly expected him to let loose an enormous belch.

Bodily secretions—the manure, the snot, the tears— were ubiquitous outside of this dignified New England home. The mound of black compost sat silently and waited for the gardener's awed veneration.

Then my dad and I piled back into the dump truck, heading home to the farm. In the cab, as we pulled out onto the narrow, winding road, my father handed me the check on which the author's enigmatic signature was drying.

"Look at that." He said it as if we had had just pulled off an epic heist and were absconding with millions of dollars worth of jewels.

"Mm, hm," I mumbled. "Right." I was a fan of Alan Moore, a comic book writer who looked like Jesus if he was slowly turning into a werewolf. And Franklin W. Dixon, in whose formulaic *Hardy Boys* mysteries I found a comforting consistency and narrative reliability that was seemingly absent from the real world. Updike, for all his accolades, had written a series of books about a middle-class man called "Rabbit." I had nothing against him, but I was decidedly uninterested in his work.

Updike hustled back into his house to write or simply bask in the adoration of the literary world. I, on the other hand, was a hostage, forced to ride along with my dad as he drove around Massachusetts delivering compost that wealthy, socialite gardeners referred to simply as "black gold." When we returned home, I galumphed upstairs to lie on my bed and, holding the comic book over me, let the colors and onomatopoeia rain down upon my head.

As I read about the inner workings of Arkham Asylum, John Updike, who was spreading manure on his garden at that moment, had 17 years left to live.

I eventually grew older. The books I read contained fewer and fewer pictures. Soon I was left with only words. I started to write my own stories, and on January 27, 2009, in a hospital not far away, Updike died of lung cancer.

Like the pile of compost we had dropped on his lawn, he became the residue of life.

EPILOGUE

A woman learns that her death is approaching at a steady, measured pace that is both apathetic and horrifying. A doctor, numb to human emotion after years of delivering such news, sits her down in a cold room without wind or sun and explains that she has, at most, seven years to live. There are treatments and procedures to endure, but in all honesty, they will only make life more miserable, and therefore easier to let go of in the end.

That night, alone in what feels like an eternal and dark stillness, with nothing but the blathering of a nearby television to distract her thoughts from the fact that she will stop thinking, her consciousness morphs into an ouroboros, a snake eating its own tail. All of her existence is focused solely on the promise of oblivion. The one is consumed, nullified, and nurtured by the other.

Nearby, an arachnid scuttles across a book cover. It is busy and unaffected by the proximity of its own death.

"It is," the woman realizes as the spider pauses on the second "b" in the word "Rabbit," "just a matter of perspective."

"I had it wrong," she says to herself, speaking aloud in her head as if explaining something of vital importance to a stranger. "Seven years is an entire lifetime for some creatures. For others it is more. How long does a spider live? A few months, maybe?"

She loves her son and her daughter and sometimes, if she tries hard enough, even her husband. But the fact that she has only seven years and they, with no specific diagnosis, have eternity, places them out of her emotional reach. They will never again experience things in the same way. They will never be on equal footing, and therefore all of her joys with them will have an unpleasant aftertaste. Looking together at a sunset, she will think to herself: "'What a beautiful sunset,' is what a person is supposed to think when they see something like this."

The next morning, without telling her children or her husband what she is doing, she drives to an animal shelter.

A young man with a single, massive eyebrow and an oddly shapeless nose tries to convince her to adopt an older dog.

"No" she says. "I'm looking for a puppy. A large-breed puppy."

She has done her research the night before, and she knows that an Irish Wolfhound, a regal and powerful and ugly beast, suffers from a host of genetic health problems and therefore has one of the shortest life expectancies of any dog. She is in luck, the woman thinks when she lays eyes on the gangly creature, smiling for a moment before remembering her own death is the reason for wanting a puppy in the first place.

The little, curly, gray puppy, a steaming pile of poorly digested kibble sitting in another corner of its concrete cage, looks up at the woman.

"This is more paperwork than I had to fill out when we bought our house," she obligatorily jokes with the man, but inside, she is desperate to stop wasting precious moments.

Eventually, in the car on the way home, she explains everything to the puppy. "You have your whole life in front of you. All of your happiness is in front of you. This is the most life you can possibly have. And I have the same amount left. I have only a sliver of my time left, but it equates to your whole life. And together, we will live an entire lifetime."

The dog, unimpressed by her logic, urinates on the seat, leaving a stain that will linger for the remainder of the minivan's existence. When they arrive home, she dares her family to say something about the dog. Her husband, afraid of wounding her emotionally following her death sentence, shrugs and attempts to affect a smile. The children leap and spin and dance with joy around the puppy, who soon wanders off to urinate in a hidden location the family will not discover for many, many years.

With her puppy, the woman feels like she is at the beginning of something immense. Together, they walk and play and think—at least, the woman does—that they have an entire life sprawled out before them.

The wolfhound quickly grows up to be lean and solid. To the touch, she feels like a primeval rock covered by a thin layer of undulating wire.

"We are in our prime," the woman thinks, quickly redirecting her train of thought when she notices maturity setting in.

One day, the woman awakens in the morning and notices the dog does not get up and beg to go outside. Instead, she chooses to sleep another hour and rest after the preceding day's exercise. Not long after that, she stumbles while trying to enter the car. Her hips, the vet explains, have developed arthritis.

At the age of three, the dog develops a portosystemic shunt. Her circulatory system is bypassing her liver, and the dog, even with treatment, passes quickly into a kind of doddering slothfulness. Her size is no longer a symbol of power and life, but rather of the fact that soon she will be not only dead, but also very big and heavy and dead as well. She becomes an avatar of the encroachment of death, and the woman cries for her.

So the woman drives to a pet store and is greeted by an orange-flecked clerk in a yellow smock and the warm smell of pine bedding and the feces of various small creatures that eat primarily hay. She picks out a baby ferret, warm and strange in her hand, and takes him home. Ferrets, or "smelly thieves," as Aristotle called them, she learned, tend to live about four years.

Soon, the ferret is skittering around her house, stealing various household objects and stashing them God knows where. When he's in a good mood, he pops up every few steps when he scurries, his back end arched high in the air. He also makes a pleased sound that an online forum for ferret owners tells her is called "dooking," which is an onomatopoeic name like the "smash" made by a comic book superhero's fist when it strikes a villain.

The ferret is like a kitten well into his middle age, when he suddenly becomes very drowsy and is diagnosed with a thyroid condition. One day, the woman sees him standing before a plaster Buddha statue on top of her dresser and she snaps a photo. In it, he looks like he is praying, nose to nose with the jolly trinket.

Sometimes the ferret, whose smell is offensive and unsettling to outsiders but comforting and alive to the woman, starts to hiccup and falls asleep very suddenly next to the massive gray dog. If they were young, it would be adorable, she thinks, because they would be gathering their energy for life. But now it is tragic, she believes, because they are both getting old and appear to be rehearsing for the stillness of death.

At the pet store, where the clerk now has two eyebrows and is not orange, she selects a baby robo dwarf hamster. While slightly disappointed by the fact that he is not bionic, she knows, based on a small sign next to his cage, that he will live an estimated three years. When she arrives home, the hamster, which is white and fluffy and disoriented, runs as if pursuing something, or possibly being pursued, out through a cracked window and dies immediately when his internal organs are popped by the tire of a passing car.

Twenty minutes, $35 and a small white lie later, a second robo dwarf hamster, this one black, is placed with significantly more assiduity into a cage in her home. His entire life is before him, but the woman soon realizes that not all lives are equal, and a robo dwarf hamster's exist-ence—while it does embody a certain simple *joie de vivre*—

does little to assuage her fear. His daily routine, which consists entirely of eating, running on a wheel, and defecating without any knowledge of the fact, does not provide the inspiration she needs to embrace her remaining days.

In a thrift shop, she comes across an old encyclopedia devoted entirely to animals. In it, sitting on a used couch in a nearby aisle, she reads about a type of spider that lives for three years, on average. It is black, green, and incredibly poisonous. It weaves webs that are considered unparalleled in the word of human art, and it was once worshipped in the jungles of Mesoamerica as a cruel deity.

She suddenly remembers the spider that scuttled across another book, four years earlier, and helped spawn this plan in the first place. So she gets one, driving four hours round trip to a shop specializing in exotic, and from the nervous behavior of the seller, possibly illegal, pets.

At home, the spider vomits on its prey, melting small animals alive before devouring them. It is a sight that makes the woman bitter for having to leave such a strange world. The spider, which she does not name, begins working on a web of baffling beauty and design. On it settle tiny, fluffy motes and flecks of dead skin and dust, as well as tiny creatures that are about to be dissolved alive. The web, she thinks to herself, is like a story. It is a narrative spun from metallic saliva.

With the spider, the woman spends yet another full lifetime. She realizes that all lives are half lives, and toward the end of her life, she finds herself engulfed by a frantic obsession, studying thousands of species, paying special attention to their average lifespans, and acquiring creature after creature as they all tumble together toward oblivion. She becomes a morbid amateur biologist, an expert in the life cycles of all things.

Over her animals, she wields incredible power, feeding them and arranging their enclosures to challenge them and vary their daily experiences. Some of them expire unexpectedly and not in accordance with their alleged lifespans. With these beings, she feels a special affinity, because she is 32 and only months from death, meaning she too has failed to meet cosmic expectations regarding her species' longevity.

As death becomes more inexorably linked to her daily activities, showing itself in her trips to the bathroom and in the gaunt specter in the mirror, she briefly tries organized religion. Seated in a house of worship that looks like a hospital waiting room, she quickly loses any faith in its efficacy. She believed she would find solace in a group of people huddled together to worship their shared bewilderment. Instead, she sees only a cluster of tone-deaf people lip-syncing to old hymns while their minds think of work and family and television.

Her mind is elsewhere, too. And mid-service she races home to be with her decaying menagerie. She carefully arranges for hospice workers to visit her toward the end, so that she will not be ripped away from her animals. When she can no longer rise from bed, her body smelling strongly of the color yellow and caramel, she hands her eldest daughter a sealed envelope containing instructions. Her daughter follows the instructions, bringing the note to the pet store where a colony of mayflies, which do not live for years or months or even days, but rather moments, is waiting. In a small glass cage, in her bedroom, the woman watches them emerge into the world, fresh and young.

"I still have a whole lifetime," she murmurs as she expires in a room dominated by old and enfeebled animals of all shapes and sizes. It is, her husband once joked quietly to a friend, like a geriatric Noah's Ark.

As she dies, the woman senses that she is being taken, being collected by a mortified demon. The deity, or demigod, or God or possibly a Jabberwocky—she never studied theology so she is not entirely sure which—has existed for billions of years. Horrified by the promise of its own demise, it has fallen into the habit of collecting lives.

The woman is part of a colony of short-lived creatures whose lives, with all their stories and Pulitzer prizes and piles of manure and sweaters and gardens and handkerchiefs, are mere moments for the great creature. A single breath ago, the demon took a man who looked like an owl and wrote stories about a person called "Rabbit." On his next inhalation, he takes the woman. And with his next, he takes me.

Matt Geiger will be dead. Long live Matt Geiger.

ACKNOWLEDGMENTS

The countless people who contributed their wisdom and their stories. Particularly Bonnie, who served as both inspiration and cover model.

The many editors who helped give these stories form and meaning.

Alex, who came up with the clever title.

Greta and Hadley, for everything.

ABOUT THE AUTHOR

Matt Geiger was born in Brunswick, Maine in 1979. His writing has appeared in countless magazines, newspapers, and literary journals. His first collection of stories and essays won First Prize in the Midwest Book Awards and was named as a Finalist in the Next Generation Indie Book Awards and the American Book Fest. He is also the winner of numerous journalism awards. He currently lives in Wisconsin with his wife and their four-year-old daughter.

You can contact Matt through his website
www.geigerbooks.com

CPSIA information can be obtained
at www.ICGtesting.com
Printed in the USA
LVHW110059261118
598225LV00005B/7/P

9 781595 986672